ANCIENT TRUST
and
ESOTERIC WISDOM

The Teachings You Were Meant to Forget

CELESTIAL CODES

© 2025 *Celestial Codes*. All rights reserved.

This book is intended for informational and educational purposes only in relation to *Ancient Truths and Esoteric Wisdom: The Teachings You Were Meant to Forget*. The publisher and author assume no responsibility for the interpretation, application, or misapplication of the information contained herein. All trademarks, symbols, and references mentioned in this book remain the property of their respective owners. This book is provided "as is," without any express or implied warranties regarding its accuracy, completeness, or the results derived from its use. Unauthorized reproduction, distribution, or transmission of this book, in whole or in part, through any medium—physical, electronic, or otherwise—is strictly prohibited without prior written permission from the publisher.

Table of Contents

Table of Contents..3

Introduction 9

Phase 1 – The Origin: Ancient Civilizations and Lost Knowledge 11

1. The Sumerians, among the oldest known civilizations, spoke of the *Anunnaki*, beings who descended from the sky to guide humanity and impart profound wisdom............. 13

2. The Sumerians possessed an impossible knowledge of the cosmos, recording a solar system with planets *invisible to the naked eye*—long before modern telescopes could confirm their existence................................... 19

3. The Egyptians inherited fragments of this ancient wisdom and encoded it into their architecture, designing pyramids with *mathematical proportions reflecting π and the Golden Ratio*..25

4. The Great Pyramid of Giza is not a random monument—it is *perfectly aligned with Orion's Belt*, mirroring a constellation revered by the Sumerians for its connection to the divine. 31

5. No human remains were ever found inside the Great Pyramid, raising the question: *was it really a tomb, or was*

it an energy device, a temple of initiation, or something even more mysterious? 39

6. The sacred geometry found in Egyptian pyramids appears identically in *Indian temples and Gothic cathedrals*, suggesting a shared knowledge spanning continents and epochs. 45

7. The *Essenes*, an ancient spiritual order, practiced healing, fasting, meditation, and studied cosmic laws—teachings that would later be deemed dangerous by religious institutions. 51

8. The *Gnostic Gospels*, unearthed in 1945, revealed an ancient understanding of *personal enlightenment* and *inner divinity*, directly contradicting the control-based doctrines of mainstream religion. 57

9. Pre-Columbian civilizations, like the *Maya*, measured time in great cycles, creating calendars that synchronized with cosmic movements in ways modern science is only beginning to understand. 63

10. The *Nazca Lines*, massive geoglyphs visible only from above, could have been *star maps, ritual symbols, or messages meant for higher entities.* 69

Phase 2 – The Veil: Destruction, Manipulation, and the Loss of Truths 73

11. The *Library of Alexandria*, the greatest repository of ancient knowledge, was *burned multiple times*, wiping out

scientific and esoteric texts that could have rewritten history 75

12. *Giordano Bruno* was executed in 1600 for declaring that the universe was infinite and that higher laws existed beyond religious dogma. 81

13. The *Knights Templar*, guardians of lost spiritual knowledge, were accused of heresy and exterminated—not just for their power, but for what they knew. 85

14. Symbols once associated with divine wisdom were *demonized*: the pentagram, once a symbol of protection, became a mark of the forbidden 89

15. The *Council of Nicaea* (325 AD) reshaped religious history, deciding which scriptures would be included in the Bible, erasing *Gnosticism, reincarnation, and teachings on spiritual autonomy.* 95

16. The *pineal gland*, called the *third eye* by the ancients, was dismissed as irrelevant by modern science—yet it is now known to produce *DMT, the "spirit molecule."* 101

17. The *All-Seeing Eye*, now embedded in modern symbols of power, was originally an esoteric sign of *spiritual enlightenment* (the *Eye of Horus*). 107

18. *Kundalini energy*, known to yogis for thousands of years and present in Western esoteric traditions, was *ridiculed* and dismissed as "new age fantasy." 113

19. *Alchemy*, once a path to the transformation of the soul, was reduced to *witchcraft* and erased from official history. 121

20. The *Vatican Archives* contain thousands of hidden texts—ancient manuscripts, apocryphal gospels, and forbidden knowledge that has never been made public. 127

Phase 3 –The Awakening: Reassembling the Fragments of Truth 131

21. *Leonardo da Vinci* wrote in reverse and encoded his works with symbols, as if he knew that certain knowledge had to be hidden from the authorities of his time. 133

22. *Nikola Tesla* declared that *the universe operates on energy, frequency, and vibration*—the same fundamental principles at the heart of ancient esoteric traditions. 139

23. The *Fibonacci sequence* and *the Golden Ratio* appear everywhere in nature and sacred architecture, revealing an *underlying order* to the universe. 145

24. The sacred sound *OM*, chanted in Eastern traditions, resonates at frequencies that *harmonize the body and mind*, reflecting the primordial vibration of creation. 151

25. *Human DNA responds to sound, emotions, and intention*—exactly as ancient spiritual teachings described the *creative power of the word*. 157

26. The *Dogon people of Mali* knew of *Sirius B*—a star invisible without telescopes—long before modern astronomy confirmed its existence. Where did this knowledge come from?... 163

27. *Gnosticism* teaches that *the material world is an illusion*, a prison created by a *Demiurge*, and that true divinity resides *within* us, not in external gods............... 169

28. The *Ouroboros*, the serpent eating its own tail, appears in ancient civilizations worldwide—evidence of a *universal hidden truth* that transcends borders and eras. 175

29. The *science of consciousness* is now catching up to ancient wisdom: quantum physics suggests that *all things are connected*, mirroring the esoteric idea of *oneness*....181

30. The *12 Universal Laws*, passed down through Hermeticism, Vedanta, Kabbalah, and Gnosticism, offer a framework for understanding *the hidden mechanics of reality.* 189

Conclusion 195

Introduction

What if everything you thought you knew about reality was just a fragment of a greater, hidden truth? What if the world around you was carefully constructed to keep you from remembering who you truly are?

For centuries, humanity has been conditioned to accept a limited version of reality—a version shaped by institutions, dogmas, and selective history. But beneath this carefully woven tapestry lies a forgotten knowledge, one that ancient civilizations once understood and guarded fiercely. It is the knowledge of how the universe truly operates, the unseen forces that govern existence, and the power that resides within each individual.

From the towering ziggurats of Sumer to the enigmatic glyphs of the Maya, from the sacred scrolls of the Essenes to the hermetic symbols encrypted in medieval cathedrals, traces of this wisdom have survived, hidden in plain sight. The pyramids of Giza were not mere tombs, but energetic structures aligned with cosmic frequencies. The gnostic texts, once deemed heretical, whispered of an inner kingdom far greater than any external power. Leonardo da Vinci encoded forbidden truths within his art, knowing that only those with eyes to see would understand.

Yet, throughout history, powerful forces have worked tirelessly to obscure and suppress this knowledge. The Library of Alexandria burned, erasing countless esoteric texts. The Inquisition silenced those who dared to speak of hidden realms. Modern education replaced ancient wisdom with materialism, dismissing the unseen dimensions of existence as mere superstition. But now, the veil is lifting.

This book is not just a collection of ideas—it is a key. A key that unlocks the door to a deeper understanding of reality, the self, and the vast interconnected web of existence. You will uncover lost teachings, decode ancient symbols, and realize truths that have been intentionally buried. Most importantly, you will begin to remember who you really are.

If you've found this book, it is not by accident. You are ready. Welcome to the truth they never wanted you to find.

Phase 1 – The Origin: Ancient Civilizations and Lost Knowledge

"The past is not dead.

In fact, it's not even past."

— William Faulkner

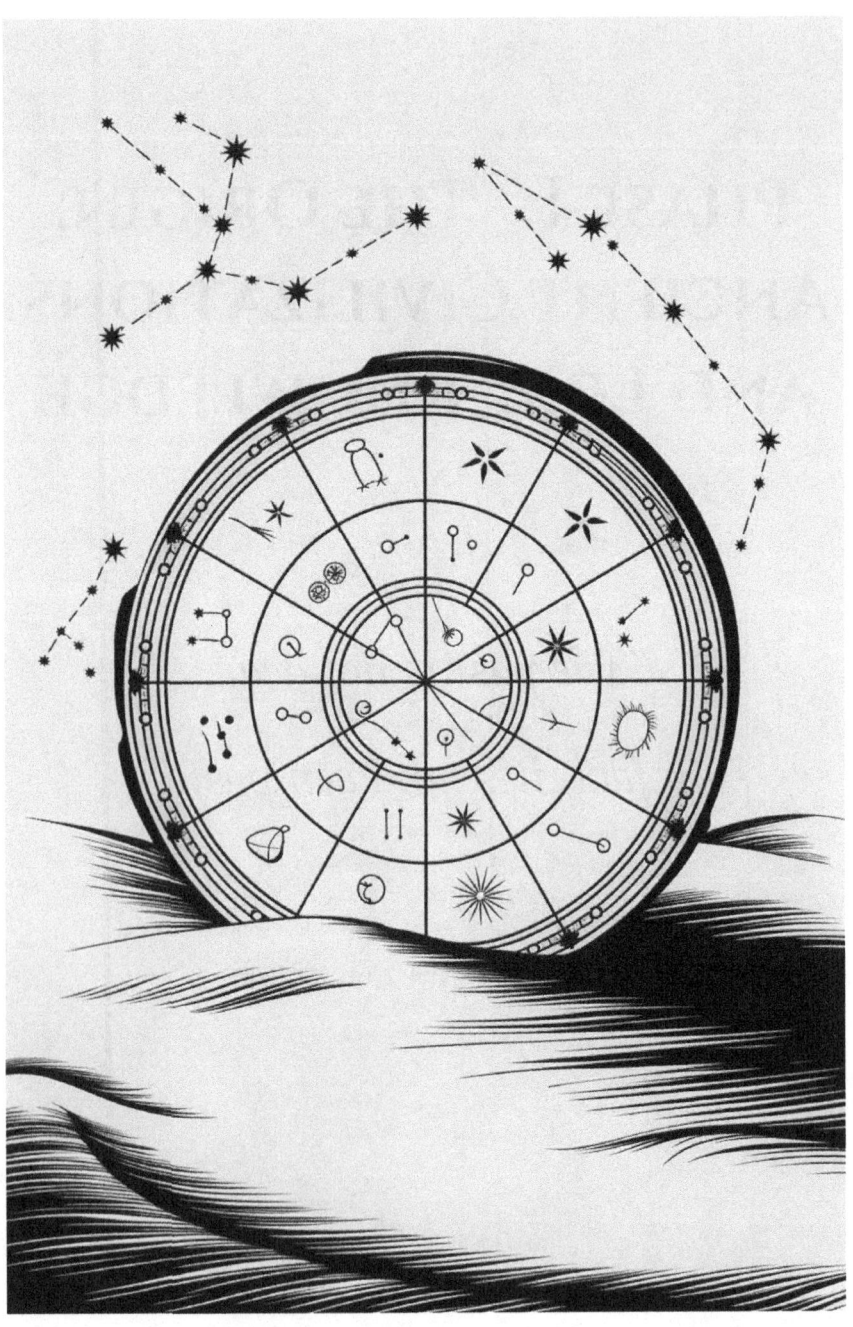

1. The Sumerians, among the oldest known civilizations, spoke of the *Anunnaki*, beings who descended from the sky to guide humanity and impart profound wisdom.

The story of human civilization is far older and more complex than we have been led to believe. Scattered among the ruins of ancient Mesopotamia, the Sumerians—the first known architects of organized society—left behind a legacy of knowledge, mythology, and history that challenges everything we think we know.

Among their many writings, one theme appears again and again: they did not claim to have built civilization on their own. They wrote of *the Anunnaki*, powerful beings who, according to their records, descended from the sky to guide humanity, shaping the foundations of early culture, governance, and knowledge. Unlike the distant and abstract gods of later religions, the Anunnaki were described with an unusual level of detail, not as mere figures of worship, but as rulers, teachers, and architects of civilization itself.

Who were these beings? Were they symbols representing cosmic forces, ancestral memories of a lost golden age, or something far more tangible—actual entities that walked among early humans, altering the trajectory of our development?

The Sumerians, whose civilization emerged suddenly and seemingly without precedent, credited the Anunnaki with gifts that propelled them far beyond their time. They introduced systems of governance, established the first legal codes, and imparted advanced knowledge of agriculture, astronomy, and mathematics. The Sumerians developed cuneiform writing—the first written language in recorded history—allegedly under the guidance of these celestial visitors.

One of the most intriguing aspects of their accounts is the specificity with which they described the Anunnaki. Unlike mythological deities of later cultures, the Sumerians depicted these beings as physical, present, and deeply involved in human affairs. They were said to have descended from *Nibiru*, a celestial body that followed an elongated orbit, bringing them into contact with Earth at specific intervals. Some texts even describe a hierarchical structure among the Anunnaki, with leaders, engineers, and advisors playing different roles in shaping the destiny of early mankind.

Many ancient cultures tell of gods descending from the heavens, but few describe these encounters with as much clarity as the Sumerians. Their tablets suggest that humanity was not left to develop on its own but was *guided*, perhaps even altered, by an external force. Were these accounts merely allegorical, or do they hint at a lost truth about our origins? The influence of the Anunnaki extended beyond government and science. They were believed to have introduced the concept of divine kingship—the idea that rulers derived their authority not from conquest alone, but from a sacred mandate. This idea persisted for millennia, shaping dynasties in Egypt, Mesopotamia, and beyond. It is no coincidence that so many ancient rulers claimed to be descendants of celestial beings.

If the Sumerian accounts are to be taken at face value, they tell a story that does not align with conventional history. A civilization that emerged suddenly, with no clear predecessors, claiming to have been instructed by sky-born beings, leaves us with profound questions. Did the Anunnaki represent a forgotten chapter of human history—one that was later erased or reinterpreted? Were they remnants of an earlier, lost civilization, their deeds later mythologized? Or could they have been something even more extraordinary?

Much of this knowledge was buried, lost to time, or deliberately suppressed. When later civilizations rose in Mesopotamia, Egypt, and beyond, many of these early accounts were fragmented, rewritten, or absorbed into broader religious traditions. The figure of the Anunnaki transformed, taking on new forms as gods and spirits, their original identity obscured.

The Sumerians, however, were clear in their beliefs. They did not see themselves as the sole architects of civilization. They remembered a time when knowledge was *given*, when powerful beings from the sky walked among them, altering the course of human history. Whether this was a symbolic retelling of natural forces, a record of a forgotten civilization, or evidence of an encounter that defies our understanding, one thing is certain—our past holds more secrets than we have been taught to believe.

The story of the Anunnaki is not just an ancient myth; it is a key, a fragment of something much larger. If we are to understand who we are and where we come from, we must look beyond the accepted narratives and into the origins of the stories themselves.

Did the Sumerians record a lost history, one that has been hidden or dismissed? Or were they merely the first to ask the same questions that still haunt us today?

2. The Sumerians possessed an impossible knowledge of the cosmos, recording a solar system with planets *invisible to the naked eye*—long before modern telescopes could confirm their existence.

The Sumerians' knowledge of the heavens was not just advanced—it was *impossibly precise* for one of the earliest known civilizations. Long before the invention of telescopes, before modern astronomy could confirm the existence of distant celestial bodies, the Sumerians documented a vision of the cosmos that defies conventional understanding.

They recorded the *solar system* with remarkable accuracy, describing planets, their movements, and even orbital details that should have been far beyond their reach. They placed the *Sun* at the center—an understanding that would not be widely accepted until Copernicus introduced the heliocentric model thousands of years later. More astonishingly, their records depicted planets *invisible to the naked eye*, including Uranus and Neptune, which modern science only confirmed in the 18th and 19th centuries.

How did they know?

If conventional history is to be believed, the Sumerians lacked the instruments necessary to observe these celestial bodies. Yet their cuneiform tablets leave little room for doubt. Were these observations made with *lost technology*, or was this knowledge *given to them*, as they themselves claimed?

One of the most intriguing artifacts is the *Akkadian Seal VA/243*, an ancient cylindrical seal that, when rolled onto clay, produces an image of what appears to be our solar system. The depiction is stunningly accurate: a central celestial body surrounded by planets, arranged much like the structure we recognize today.

The Sumerians clearly identified:

The *Sun* at the center, rather than the Earth—a concept that should have been completely unknown at the time.

Mercury, Venus, Earth, Mars, Jupiter, Saturn, Uranus, Neptune, and Pluto, all positioned relative to the Sun.

A mysterious *twelfth celestial body*, which they called *Nibiru*, said to follow an elongated orbit that brings it into the inner solar system only once every thousands of years.

At the time this seal was created, humans should have had *no way of knowing* about Uranus or Neptune. Uranus was officially discovered in 1781, Neptune in 1846, and Pluto in 1930. How, then, did the Sumerians include them in their depictions thousands of years earlier?

Some scholars dismiss this seal as symbolic rather than literal, suggesting that it may simply represent celestial gods. But the

Sumerians were not merely artists; they were meticulous *record-keepers*, documenting observations with extraordinary precision. The likelihood that they simply *guessed* the existence and positions of multiple celestial bodies strains credibility.

Their texts also reference *Nibiru*, a planet they described as part of our solar system but following a highly elliptical orbit. The Sumerians believed it was the home of the *Anunnaki*, celestial beings who imparted knowledge to early humans. Some theorists suggest that Nibiru is a *rogue planet* or *brown dwarf* with an irregular trajectory, while others believe it is *a metaphor* for something deeper—perhaps interdimensional travel or an ancient understanding of cosmic cycles.

Regardless of interpretation, one thing is certain: the Sumerians believed Nibiru was real, and its influence on Earth was significant. Could this be a relic of a forgotten cosmology, a glimpse into a deeper reality modern science has yet to uncover?

The Sumerians did not merely observe the heavens—they *calculated* them with astonishing accuracy. They recorded the *precession of the equinoxes*, a slow movement of Earth's axis that takes approximately 25,920 years to complete—a phenomenon that should have taken millennia to track. They referenced *the Saros cycle*, the precise 18-year pattern of eclipses, long before modern astronomers mapped it. Their planetary calculations deviated only slightly from those of today's advanced models.

This level of understanding suggests either *systematic observation over thousands of years* or *inherited knowledge from an earlier, lost civilization*.

The idea of celestial knowledge being *passed down* is not unique to the Sumerians. Many ancient cultures claim their astronomical wisdom was *gifted* to them rather than independently discovered. The *Egyptians* encoded advanced celestial alignments into the Great Pyramid of Giza. The *Dogon tribe of Mali* accurately described *Sirius B*, a white dwarf star invisible without modern telescopes, claiming their knowledge came from beings known as the *Nommo*. The *Maya and Aztecs* created calendars so precise that they tracked planetary cycles with astonishing accuracy.

Were these cultures all independently reaching the same conclusions, or were they receiving fragments of *a lost system of knowledge*?

If the Sumerians possessed knowledge of the solar system that surpassed their time, why was so much of it forgotten? One possibility is that as empires rose and fell, knowledge was *erased, hidden, or deliberately suppressed*. The destruction of ancient texts—like the burning of the *Library of Alexandria*—robbed humanity of untold scientific and cosmological insights.

But there may be another reason: *control*.

Knowledge is power. Civilizations that understood the cosmic order may have wielded *influence over nature and reality* in ways that modern institutions struggle to explain. If such knowledge had persisted, it could have *challenged religious and political hierarchies*, undermining those who sought to dictate the course of history.

The Sumerians left behind *a cosmic blueprint*, a map of the universe that should not have been possible for their era. Whether through inherited wisdom, forgotten technology, or external intervention, they possessed *a knowledge of the heavens that modern science is only now beginning to grasp.* What else have we lost? What other truths lie buried beneath the weight of history, waiting to be unearthed?

The time has come to *question everything we assume about the past.* The knowledge of the ancients has not disappeared—it has simply been *obscured, waiting for those willing to see beyond the veil.*

Did the Sumerians glimpse a truth we are only now rediscovering? Or were they the last keepers of a wisdom far older than history itself?

3. The Egyptians inherited fragments of this ancient wisdom and encoded it into their architecture, designing pyramids with *mathematical proportions reflecting π and the Golden Ratio.*

The Egyptians did not merely build monuments; they encoded *a cosmic language* into stone—structures that still defy conventional explanations. Towering above the sands of Giza, the Great Pyramid stands as a silent testament to *a forgotten knowledge*, a wisdom so advanced that even modern engineering struggles to replicate it. Official history tells us that these pyramids were mere royal tombs, constructed through brute labor and primitive tools. But as we unravel the mathematical precision and celestial alignments embedded within their design, another possibility emerges: the ancient Egyptians were not simply builders—they were inheritors of an *esoteric science* that stretched back to an unknown source.

The Great Pyramid of Giza, the most famous of these enigmatic structures, was not thrown together through guesswork. Its dimensions reflect a mastery of mathematics that should have been far beyond the capabilities of a civilization over 4,500 years ago. Its height-to-base ratio is a near-perfect representation of π *(pi)*—the mathematical constant essential to understanding circles, waves, and universal harmonics. The structure encodes *the Golden Ratio (φ)*, a proportion found throughout nature, from the spirals of galaxies to the growth patterns of plants and even the human body. If you divide the perimeter of the pyramid by twice its height, you get a number nearly identical to *π (3.14159)*—an astonishing coincidence, if indeed it was unintentional. The longitude of the Great Pyramid aligns almost exactly with the speed of light (*299,792,458 m/s*), an eerie correlation that challenges conventional history.

How could an ancient civilization, without advanced tools or measuring devices, construct a monument that encodes such precise mathematical and physical constants? Was this knowledge independently discovered, or did the Egyptians inherit it from a far older, forgotten source?

The pyramids of Egypt were deliberately aligned with the cosmos. The Great Pyramid is perfectly oriented to *true north*, with an error margin of just 1/15th of a degree—an accuracy that modern builders can only achieve with the most sophisticated instruments. The three pyramids at Giza mirror the *Orion's Belt* constellation, aligning with the brightest stars of Orion as they appeared in the sky thousands of years ago. The descending passage of the Great Pyramid is precisely aligned with the *North Star*. The layout of the entire Giza plateau corresponds to the *Earthly projection of the sky*, as if the pyramids were built to reflect the heavens.

Ancient texts from multiple civilizations suggest that Orion was *a gateway to the divine*, a celestial origin point for higher beings. Did the Egyptians build their monuments as a means to connect with these cosmic forces, or were they following an architectural blueprint left by an earlier, lost civilization?

Mainstream archaeology insists that the pyramids were built as tombs for pharaohs, yet no mummies have ever been found inside the Great Pyramid. Unlike other royal burial sites, *there are no inscriptions, elaborate wall paintings, or traditional funerary markers.* Instead, we find something even more intriguing. The so-called *King's Chamber* contains a mysterious granite box that some researchers suggest once housed *a lost energy device.* The interior structure resembles the *resonance chambers* of modern acoustic systems, designed to amplify and direct sound waves. The material composition of the pyramid—limestone, granite, and basalt—shares similarities with conductive materials used in *energy transmission.*

Could it be that the pyramids were not tombs, but *power stations of an ancient energy system*, utilizing frequencies and vibrations in ways we are only beginning to understand? Nikola Tesla once theorized about *wireless energy transmission*, and the Great Pyramid's construction bears an uncanny resemblance to his own experimental towers.

Egypt was not the only civilization to build pyramids with astronomical and mathematical precision. Strikingly similar structures exist in multiple cultures across the globe. The pyramids of Teotihuacan in Mexico align with *celestial events* just as precisely as those in Egypt. The step pyramids of China, largely forgotten by history, exhibit measurements that mirror those of Giza. The Bosnian pyramids, though controversial, show underground tunnels and electromagnetic anomalies similar to those theorized at Giza.

Did these cultures independently come to the same conclusions, or were they all heirs to a single, ancient system of knowledge—one that was lost and fragmented over time?

Greek philosopher Plato, in his dialogues *Timaeus* and *Critias*, spoke of Atlantis, a highly advanced civilization that vanished in a great catastrophe. He described its people as *masters of architecture, mathematics, and cosmic wisdom*— a description eerily reminiscent of the Egyptians. Some researchers suggest that Egypt was a surviving colony of this lost civilization, preserving fragments of its knowledge in stone. The *Zep Tepi* ("First Time"), an Egyptian myth, tells of an era when *gods walked among men*, bringing civilization and wisdom. Could this "golden age" refer to a time when advanced beings—whether extraterrestrial, interdimensional, or remnants of a prior human civilization—guided early humanity?

Despite overwhelming evidence of mathematical precision, astronomical knowledge, and possible energy applications, mainstream academia continues to downplay the true significance of the pyramids. Why? Some theories suggest that acknowledging the *true purpose of the pyramids* would force a complete rewrite of history, one that questions:

The *timeline* of human civilization—were there *advanced cultures before those we officially recognize*?

The true *nature of ancient wisdom*—was knowledge *handed down*, rather than gradually developed?

The *possibility of lost sciences*—could there have been forms of technology based on resonance, energy fields, or frequencies that we have yet to rediscover?

The Great Pyramid of Giza is not just a monument—it is *a message*, a mathematical and cosmic code left behind by those who came before us. Whether they were *human visionaries, interdimensional teachers, or inheritors of a lost civilization*, their legacy endures in these ancient structures.

It is time to question everything we assume about the past. The pyramids were not merely royal tombs; they were *beacons of knowledge*, built to stand the test of time, waiting for those with eyes to see.

Their message is clear: the answers to our deepest mysteries are *hidden in plain sight*, encoded in stone, waiting to be unlocked.

4. The Great Pyramid of Giza is not a random monument—it is *perfectly aligned with Orion's Belt,* mirroring a constellation revered by the Sumerians for its connection to the divine.

The Great Pyramid of Giza is not merely an architectural wonder; it is a message written in stone, encoded with secrets that modern science is only beginning to unravel. Among its most astonishing features is its *alignment with Orion's Belt*, a constellation revered by the Egyptians as the celestial manifestation of Osiris, the god of the afterlife and resurrection. But this connection is not unique to Egypt. The Sumerians, thousands of years earlier, also held Orion in deep significance, linking it to divine beings who descended from the heavens.

Why did these ancient civilizations—separated by time and geography—consider Orion so important? Was it simply a cultural coincidence, or did they inherit a shared knowledge of a deeper cosmic truth?

The pyramids at Giza are not randomly placed; their positions mirror the three bright stars of Orion's Belt—Alnitak, Alnilam, and Mintaka. This alignment is so precise that it suggests the builders had an advanced understanding of astronomy, far beyond what should have been possible for a civilization over 4,500 years ago.

The correlation between Orion and the pyramids was first brought to light by researchers who noticed that the stars of Orion's Belt do not form a perfect line but a slightly offset diagonal. The layout of the pyramids follows this same pattern, with the smallest pyramid, Menkaure, positioned slightly out of alignment with the others—just as Mintaka appears slightly off in the night sky. This was not an accident. Further evidence of this cosmic blueprint lies in the shafts within the Great Pyramid. These narrow passages, originally thought to be ventilation ducts, are precisely angled to point toward specific stars. The southern shaft of the King's Chamber aligns almost perfectly with *Alnitak*, the brightest star in Orion's Belt, while the northern shaft points to *Thuban*, a star in the Draco constellation that was once the North Star during Egypt's ancient past.

What was the purpose of these alignments? Some theorists suggest that the shafts were meant to serve as pathways for the pharaoh's soul, guiding it back to the celestial realm of Osiris. But others propose a far more provocative idea—were the pyramids built as a form of communication, a beacon designed to connect with something beyond our world?

The Egyptians were not the only ancient civilization obsessed with Orion. Thousands of years earlier, the Sumerians also held this constellation in great reverence, associating it with Anu, the supreme sky god.

Sumerian texts speak of the *Anunnaki*, celestial beings who descended from the heavens to guide and shape early human civilization. Some interpretations suggest that these beings were believed to have *originated* from Orion. If so, this raises an even greater question—did the Egyptians encode Orion into their most sacred structures as a tribute to the same celestial figures the Sumerians worshipped?

The name *Osiris* itself may hold a hidden clue. Some researchers have noted that the root of the name bears linguistic similarities to *Asar* or *Ausar*, possibly linking it to older Mesopotamian traditions. Was Osiris a reimagined version of an ancient figure that predated Egyptian civilization, one whose origins were tied to the sky?

One of the most astonishing aspects of the Orion-Pyramid correlation is that the alignment was *most precise around 10,500 BCE*—far earlier than the time mainstream archaeology claims the pyramids were built. This has led some researchers to suggest that the pyramids may be far older than we think, possibly the remnants of a lost civilization that existed long before the rise of dynastic Egypt.

The reason this date is significant lies in the astronomical phenomenon known as *precession*. Over a cycle of approximately 26,000 years, Earth's axial tilt slowly shifts, altering the position of the stars relative to our planet. Around

10,500 BCE, Orion's Belt would have been in its lowest position in the sky, aligning perfectly with the pyramids.

Did the builders of Giza encode this information deliberately? If so, it implies that they either possessed knowledge of precession—something historians claim was only discovered by the Greeks thousands of years later—or that the pyramids were constructed *during* that period, pushing the origins of Egyptian civilization back by millennia.

If this theory is correct, it suggests that the Great Pyramid is not just a tomb or a monument, but a time marker, a message left behind by an earlier civilization.

Beyond its stellar alignments, the Great Pyramid exhibits another strange characteristic: its internal structure suggests that it was designed to resonate with frequencies that match natural harmonics found in the Earth and the cosmos. The use of limestone and granite—materials known for their conductive properties—has led some to theorize that the pyramid was not just an astronomical marker but also an energy device.

The concept of *pyramid power* has been widely debated, but recent studies have shown that the Great Pyramid can focus electromagnetic energy within its chambers. Could this be related to the idea of Orion as a source of cosmic energy? Did the ancients believe that by aligning their structures to Orion, they could harness some form of celestial force?

The concept of ancient structures resonating with cosmic frequencies is not unique to Egypt. Many megalithic sites around the world, from Stonehenge to the Mayan temples, exhibit properties that suggest they were built with a sophisticated understanding of sound and energy. The question is—where did this knowledge come from?

The connection between Orion, the Sumerians, and the Egyptians may not be a coincidence. It hints at a lost system of knowledge, one that was shared across civilizations but later fragmented and obscured by time. The pyramids of Giza are not isolated anomalies; they are part of a much larger pattern—one that suggests our ancestors were aware of a cosmic relationship that modern science has yet to fully comprehend.

If Orion was considered the place of origin for divine beings, and if its alignment with the Great Pyramid was intentional, then we must ask: what were the ancient Egyptians trying to communicate? Were they honoring their gods, or were they marking a location of *real* significance—one that holds a deeper connection to our own origins?

The more we study these ancient alignments, the more we are forced to reconsider the nature of history itself. The Great Pyramid may be far more than a tomb; it may be a *celestial gateway*, a mathematical time capsule pointing to a truth we have long forgotten.

Perhaps Orion is not just a constellation. Perhaps it is a message, waiting to be deciphered.

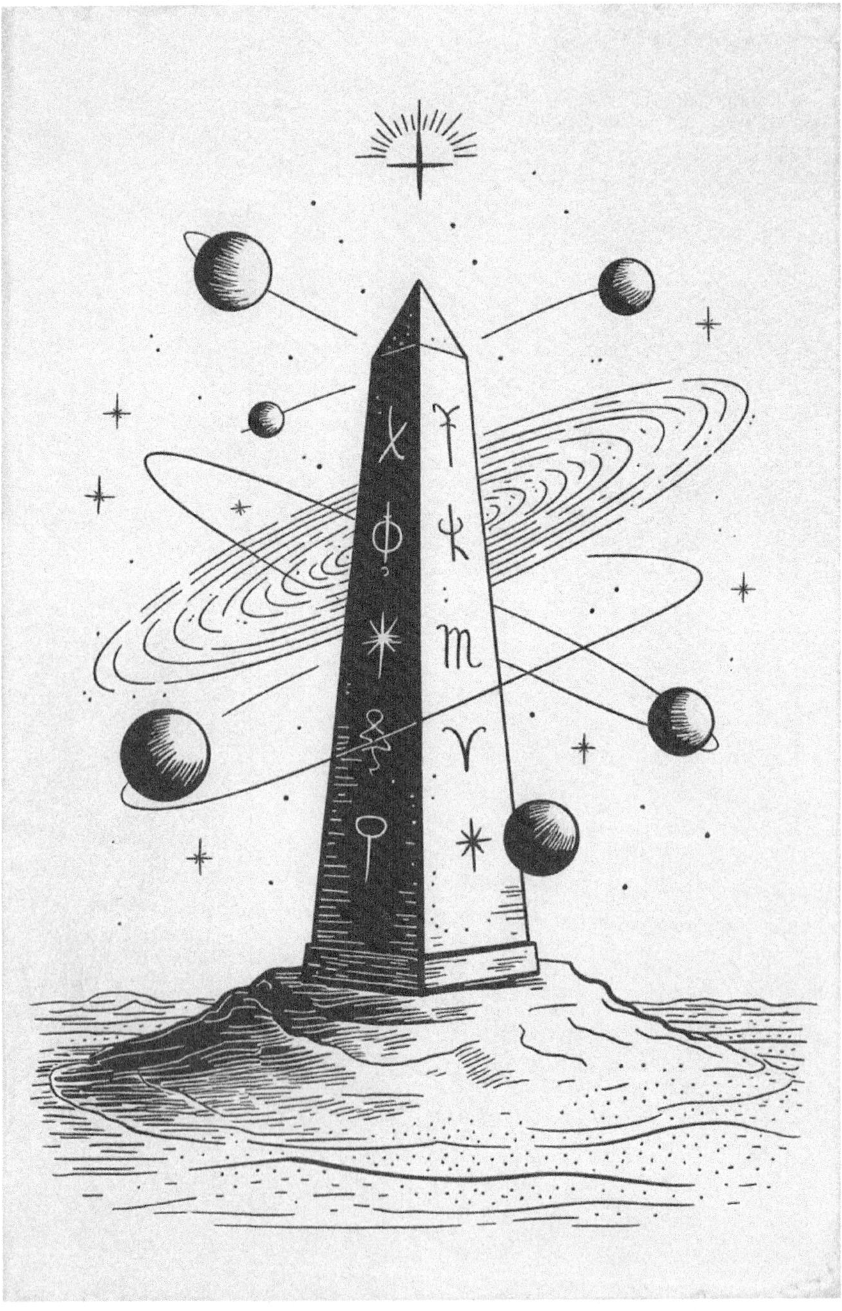

5. No human remains were ever found inside the Great Pyramid, raising the question: *was it really a tomb, or was it an energy device, a temple of initiation, or something even more mysterious?*

For centuries, the Great Pyramid of Giza has been assumed to be a royal tomb, built to house the remains of a powerful pharaoh on his journey to the afterlife. Yet, despite exhaustive explorations, *no human remains have ever been found inside.* Unlike other burial chambers in Egypt—filled with intricate inscriptions, ornate sarcophagi, and elaborate offerings—this colossal structure stands eerily empty.

If the Great Pyramid was truly intended as a tomb, why does it lack the fundamental elements of an Egyptian burial site? Why is there not a single hieroglyph carved into its walls, no funerary texts, no depictions of gods guiding the deceased? Even in pyramids of lesser importance, royal burials were marked with clear indications of their purpose. The absence of such evidence in the Great Pyramid raises an unavoidable question: *was it ever meant to be a tomb at all?*

Some researchers propose an alternative explanation—one that challenges the conventional historical narrative. Could it be that the Great Pyramid was something else entirely? Was it *a machine, a temple of initiation, or even a conduit of energy?*

The so-called *King's Chamber*, deep within the structure, contains nothing but a massive granite box, crudely cut and without decoration. Egyptologists refer to it as a sarcophagus, yet no lid has ever been found, and its size suggests that it may have served a function beyond burial. The material used—rose granite from Aswan—is known for its high quartz content, a natural conductor of energy. Some theorists suggest that this chamber was designed *not to house a body, but to resonate with frequencies*, amplifying energies in ways that modern science is only beginning to explore.

Further fueling speculation is the design of the pyramid itself. Unlike other Egyptian tombs, which were constructed with a descending passage leading to an underground burial chamber, the Great Pyramid features a series of passages that seem to *channel movement upward*, culminating in the so-called Grand Gallery—a corridor whose shape and proportions bear an uncanny resemblance to *acoustic resonance chambers*. Could it be that these structures were not meant for the dead, but for the *living*?

Some believe that the Great Pyramid served as a center for *mystical initiation*, a place where individuals underwent a transformation of consciousness rather than a physical burial. In this theory, the granite box within the King's Chamber was not a sarcophagus, but a chamber designed to alter perception, induce altered states of awareness, and connect the initiate with higher realms.

Others suggest that the pyramid was part of a lost energy system—an ancient power plant of sorts, harnessing telluric currents from the Earth and cosmic energy from the stars. The materials used in its construction, including the conductive properties of granite and the insulating properties of limestone, support this idea. The theory is further reinforced by the fact that the *original casing stones*, now mostly missing, were made of polished Tura limestone, which could have once acted as an insulator, preventing energy from dissipating.

Nikola Tesla, the visionary scientist who experimented with *wireless energy transmission*, built one of his experimental towers with a strikingly similar geometric principle. He believed that energy could be extracted directly from the Earth's natural electrical charge and transmitted wirelessly. Could it be that the ancients understood these principles thousands of years before modern civilization?

The mystery deepens when considering the work of explorers who have reported strange phenomena within the pyramid— unusual electromagnetic fields, heightened states of awareness, and even accounts of minor physiological effects after spending time inside the chambers.

If the Great Pyramid was not merely a tomb, but a structure designed for *energy, initiation, or something beyond our understanding*, what does that say about the true level of knowledge possessed by the ancient builders?

Perhaps history has misinterpreted the purpose of this monument. Perhaps it was never meant to preserve the dead, but to *transform the living*.

And if that is true, then what else have we misunderstood?

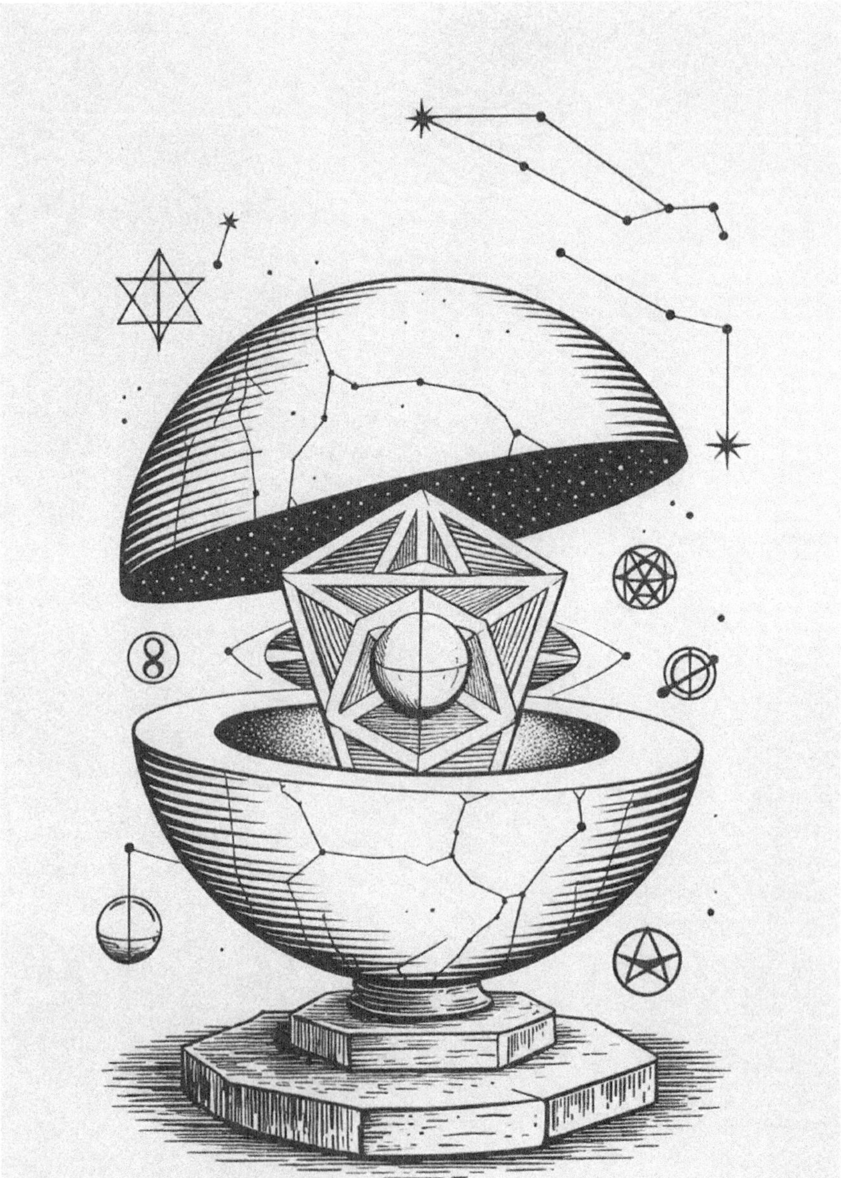

6. The sacred geometry found in Egyptian pyramids appears identically in *Indian temples and Gothic cathedrals,* suggesting a shared knowledge spanning continents and epochs.

Across the world, from the towering pyramids of Egypt to the intricate temples of India and the grand cathedrals of Europe, a silent language is embedded in stone. A language of *sacred geometry*, encoded in structures that defy time, geography, and cultural boundaries. How is it that civilizations separated by vast distances, with no apparent contact, built their most sacred sites using *the same mathematical principles*? Could it be that they were drawing from a shared, forgotten knowledge—one that existed long before recorded history?

The Great Pyramid of Giza is an architectural masterpiece, not just in size but in precision. Its proportions encode π *(pi)* and φ *(the Golden Ratio)*, fundamental constants found throughout nature. These same proportions appear in the design of Indian temples, in the intricate carvings of Angkor Wat, and even in the soaring Gothic cathedrals of medieval Europe.

But sacred geometry is more than just aesthetics—it is a blueprint that reflects the underlying patterns of the universe. The Golden Ratio, also known as *divine proportion*, appears in the spirals of galaxies, the branching of trees, the proportions of the human body, and the frequencies of sound. If nature follows these mathematical principles, is it possible that ancient architects understood them as well, using them to create structures that resonated with cosmic forces?

In India, the *Sri Yantra*—a sacred geometric diagram used in Hindu and Buddhist traditions—mirrors the same mathematical ratios found in Egyptian pyramids. Its interlocking triangles represent the union of opposing forces, much like the balance of dualities seen in Hermetic and alchemical teachings. Similarly, the towering spires of Gothic cathedrals, reaching toward the heavens, follow the same geometric ratios encoded in the Great Pyramid.

One of the most fascinating connections between these structures is the use of *resonance and sound frequencies*. Studies have shown that many ancient temples and cathedrals were designed to *amplify and channel sound waves*, much like modern acoustic chambers. The King's Chamber in the Great Pyramid, for example, has been theorized to resonate at specific frequencies, while the high-vaulted ceilings of European cathedrals were designed to enhance the power of Gregorian chants. Could these buildings have been constructed *not just for visual grandeur, but for energetic transformation*?

If sacred geometry was used to create places of worship, meditation, and initiation across different civilizations, where did this knowledge originate? Was it independently discovered, or did it stem from an ancient, pre-existing tradition that predates known history? Some researchers believe that this wisdom may have come from a *forgotten civilization*, a lost era in which humanity possessed a deeper understanding of the connection between space, energy, and consciousness.

The geometric symbols that appear in Egyptian temples, Indian mandalas, and medieval cathedral layouts are strikingly similar. They encode *Fibonacci sequences, spirals, and star patterns* that mimic celestial alignments. Were these cultures simply following intuitive artistic expression, or were they intentionally embedding *universal mathematical truths* into their sacred sites?

Mainstream archaeology suggests that civilizations developed in isolation, with no direct exchange of architectural ideas. Yet, the undeniable parallels between these structures suggest otherwise. How did cultures separated by thousands of miles arrive at the same geometric conclusions? Could it be that this knowledge was passed down through a hidden lineage—one that has since been lost or deliberately obscured?

If the builders of the past encoded these mathematical principles into their most sacred sites, *what were they trying to communicate?* Were they preserving knowledge for future generations, knowing that one day we might begin to rediscover the truths hidden within their architecture?

Perhaps these structures were not just monuments, but *gateways*—portals into a forgotten science, a map leading us back to an understanding that has been buried beneath the sands of time.

The real question is: are we ready to see it?

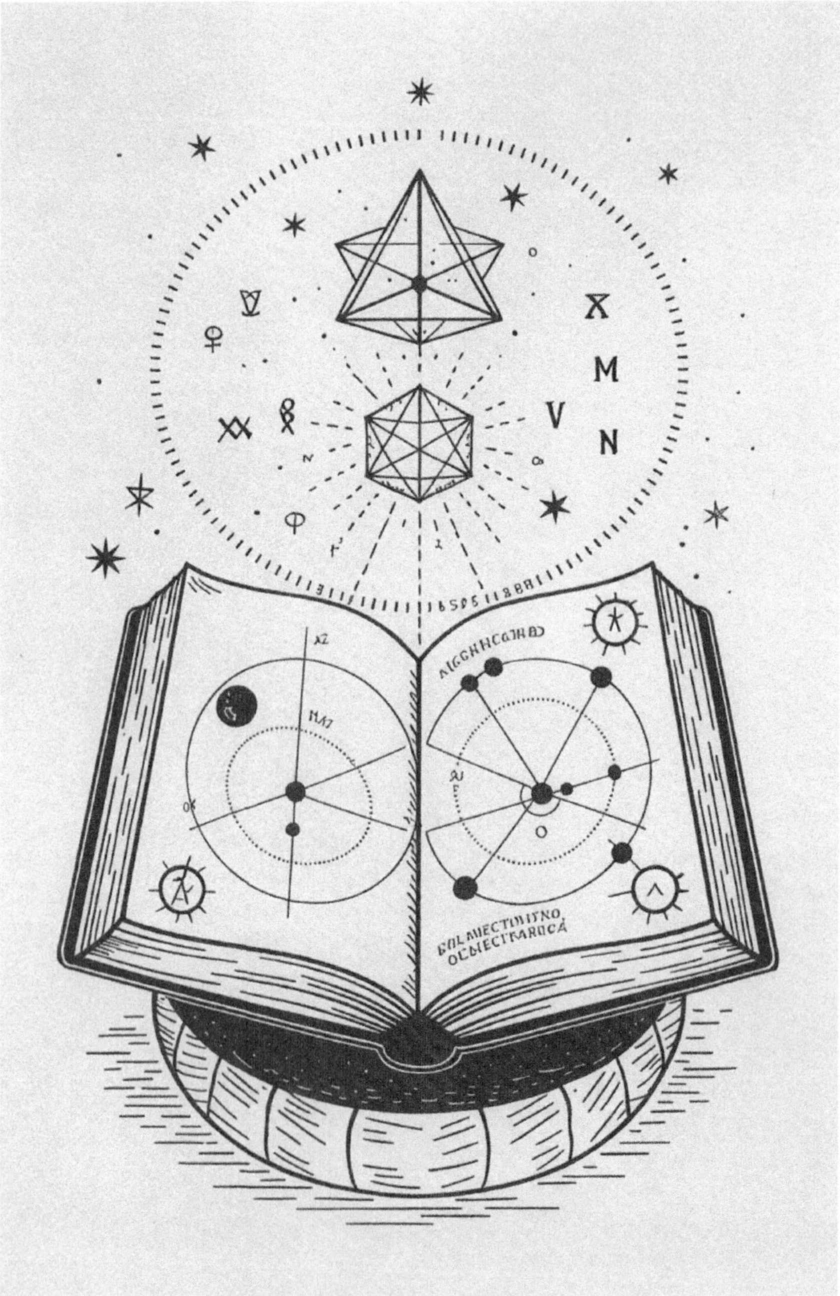

7. The *Essenes*, an ancient spiritual order, practiced healing, fasting, meditation, and studied cosmic laws—teachings that would later be deemed dangerous by religious institutions.

Hidden away in the desert, far from the centers of power and corruption, a mysterious spiritual order existed long before the rise of institutionalized religion. The *Essenes* were not merely an isolated sect—they were seekers of truth, preservers of sacred knowledge, and practitioners of ancient wisdom that would later be deemed *dangerous* by those who sought control.

Who were they? And why were their teachings, which emphasized healing, meditation, fasting, and the study of cosmic laws, seen as a threat?

Unlike the ruling religious institutions of their time, the Essenes believed that true enlightenment did not come through external rituals or obedience to a priestly class, but through an *inner transformation*—a direct connection between the individual and the universe itself. They lived apart from society, adhering to strict spiritual disciplines designed to purify the body and mind, unlocking states of awareness that mainstream religion would later suppress.

They practiced *fasting*, not as a mere act of self-denial, but as a way to recalibrate their connection to the cosmos. They engaged in *meditation*, not simply as a form of relaxation, but as a method to access higher states of consciousness. They studied *healing* as an integration of the physical and the spiritual, recognizing that disease was not just a condition of the body, but an imbalance of the soul.

But perhaps the most controversial aspect of their teachings was their understanding of *cosmic laws*. The Essenes believed that the universe was governed by principles that extended beyond human law—principles that connected all things through vibration, frequency, and energy. They saw these laws reflected in nature, the stars, and the cycles of time, long before such ideas would be echoed in the fields of quantum physics and metaphysics.

Their knowledge was not confined to the physical world. They studied *the nature of the soul, the cycles of reincarnation, and the illusion of material existence*. They spoke of the *hidden teachings of the prophets*—wisdom that was stripped away from official religious texts and locked behind the walls of power.

If their philosophy was so profound, why were they erased from mainstream history?

The answer lies in what they *represented*. The Essenes were a challenge to religious and political structures because they emphasized *spiritual sovereignty*. They taught that enlightenment was not something that could be granted by an institution or bestowed through ritual, but something that each individual could attain through direct experience. This was dangerous to those who sought to control the narrative of spiritual truth.

Much of what we know about the Essenes comes from the *Dead Sea Scrolls*, ancient texts discovered in the caves of Qumran in 1947. These documents revealed a hidden spiritual tradition that had been erased from religious doctrine—a tradition that spoke of higher knowledge, divine laws, and an esoteric path to awakening. The scrolls also contained references to *secret teachings of Jesus*, which diverged from the version of his life later constructed by religious authorities. Was Jesus himself an Essene? Many researchers believe so. His teachings on love, healing, and the kingdom of heaven *within* align closely with Essene philosophy. His acts of healing were not just miracles, but applications of deeper knowledge—knowledge that the Essenes had preserved for centuries. If Jesus was indeed connected to this tradition, it would explain why many of his words were later altered, removed, or reinterpreted by the early Church.

But the Essenes were not the only group to carry this hidden wisdom. Their practices bore striking similarities to *Eastern spiritual traditions*, suggesting a possible exchange of knowledge between different parts of the ancient world. Their ideas of purification, breathwork, and vibrational healing resonate with the teachings of Indian yogis, Taoist masters, and Gnostic sages.

If these connections exist, then the Essenes were not just a forgotten sect of Judaism. They were part of a greater, global lineage of *esoteric wisdom*, stretching back to civilizations far older than history acknowledges.

But history is written by those who hold power. Over time, the Essenes disappeared from public record. Their teachings were either suppressed or absorbed into religious structures in a diluted form. What remains today are fragments—whispers of a path that once led seekers toward true self-mastery.

Yet their influence lingers. Their knowledge did not vanish; it simply went underground, passed down through secret traditions, mystical orders, and hidden texts. And now, as we begin to piece together the lost fragments of ancient wisdom, the teachings of the Essenes may be more relevant than ever.

Were they the last guardians of a forgotten science—one that bridged the gap between spirituality and the unseen forces of the cosmos? Or were they simply one of many groups who understood that reality is far greater than what we have been led to believe?

Perhaps their greatest secret is not what they knew, but *why* their knowledge was taken from us.

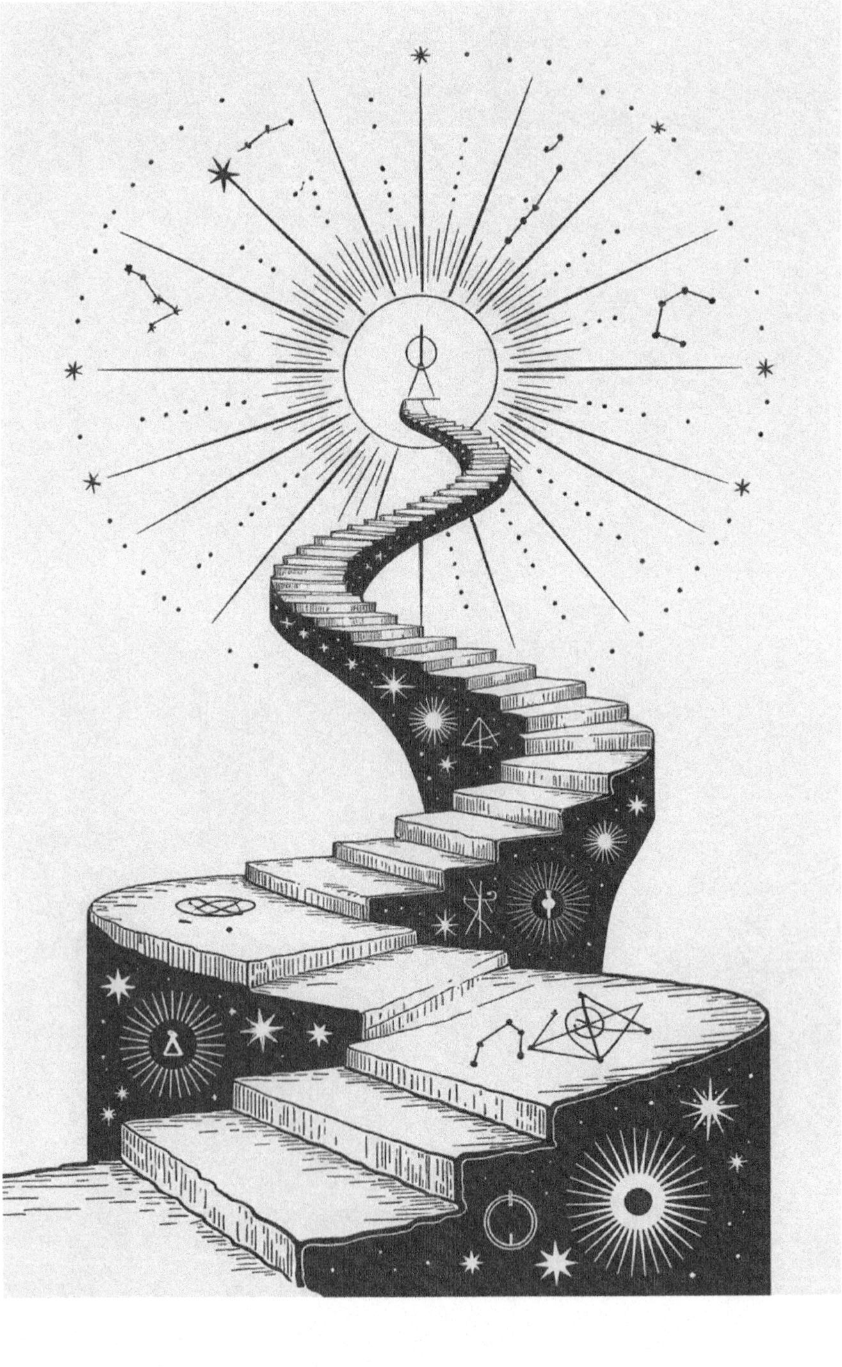

8. The *Gnostic Gospels,* unearthed in 1945, revealed an ancient understanding of *personal enlightenment* and *inner divinity,* directly contradicting the control-based doctrines of mainstream religion.

In 1945, buried in the sands of Nag Hammadi, Egypt, a discovery was made that threatened to unravel centuries of religious control. Hidden away in sealed clay jars, untouched for nearly two millennia, were *the Gnostic Gospels*—a collection of ancient texts that presented an entirely different vision of spirituality. Unlike the dogmatic teachings that had shaped institutionalized religion, these writings spoke of *personal enlightenment, inner divinity, and the illusion of external authority.*

Why were these texts hidden? And why were their teachings so dangerous to the powers that sought to define spiritual truth?

The Gnostics, unlike mainstream religious followers, did not see divinity as something external, nor did they believe that salvation required an intermediary. They taught that *the divine spark* existed within every human being and that enlightenment was not granted by institutions, but *discovered within oneself.* This idea directly contradicted the hierarchical structures of organized religion, which built their authority on the notion that spiritual access required priesthoods, rituals, and obedience to sacred laws.

The central theme of Gnostic thought was *gnosis*—a term meaning *direct experiential knowledge of the divine.* This was not faith in doctrine, but a deep, personal understanding of the nature of reality. The Gnostics believed that human beings were trapped in an illusion—a material world created not by a benevolent god, but by an imposter, a *Demiurge*, who sought to blind humanity to its true nature. This *Demiurge*, sometimes identified with the god of the Old Testament, was portrayed as an entity that desired control, demanding worship and submission rather than wisdom and awakening.

If the material world was a prison, then the path to liberation lay in *self-discovery*, not in obedience to religious law. The Gnostic Gospels painted an entirely different picture of Jesus—not as a messianic figure who came to establish a church, but as a *spiritual teacher*, one who revealed the hidden knowledge necessary to break free from illusion. In texts like *The Gospel of Thomas*, Jesus does not command worship; instead, he says: *"The kingdom of God is inside you, and all around you. Split a piece of wood, and I am there. Lift a stone, and you will find me."*

This was not the message that religious authorities wanted to preserve. A spirituality that empowered individuals to seek truth directly—without temples, rituals, or priestly intermediaries—posed a threat to the growing institutions of control. It is no coincidence that, in the early centuries of Christianity, the Gnostics were *branded as heretics, hunted down, and silenced.* Their books were destroyed, their knowledge erased, and their teachings buried—literally and figuratively.

But the discovery at Nag Hammadi changed everything. Suddenly, long-suppressed wisdom was available once more, revealing the extent to which spiritual history had been rewritten. These texts shed light on ideas that had survived only in fragments—concepts of *reincarnation, divine feminine energy, and the illusory nature of time and space,* all of which had been stripped from mainstream theology.

One of the most striking aspects of the Gnostic Gospels is their emphasis on *Sophia*, the divine embodiment of wisdom. Unlike traditional Christian teachings, which often presented God as an external male figure, Gnosticism acknowledged the necessity of both *masculine and feminine* aspects of the divine. Sophia was seen as the creative force behind the universe, a principle of enlightenment that had been lost due to the Demiurge's deception. This recognition of *divine feminine energy* directly contradicted patriarchal religious structures, which sought to remove the feminine aspect from spiritual practice.

If the teachings of the Gnostic Gospels had been widely accepted, how different would history have been? Without rigid hierarchies, would humanity have been free to explore consciousness without restriction? Without the fear-based doctrines of sin and damnation, would society have evolved toward enlightenment rather than control?

The suppression of the Gnostic texts was not merely a battle over theology—it was an effort to maintain *power over the mind and soul*. A world where individuals understood their own divine nature would be impossible to rule through fear. It would be a world without religious oppression, without manipulation through guilt, and without dependence on external saviors.

Yet, despite centuries of suppression, the ideas within the Gnostic Gospels *never truly disappeared*. They resurfaced in the mystical traditions of the Sufis, in the hidden teachings of the Kabbalah, in the practices of esoteric Christianity, and even in modern spiritual movements that emphasize *inner awakening over blind faith*.

What the discovery of these texts proves is that *truth has a way of surviving, even in the face of relentless erasure*. The questions they raise remain as relevant today as they were two thousand years ago:

- If the divine is within us, why have we been taught to seek it outside?

- If enlightenment is a personal journey, why have institutions claimed ownership of it?
- And if reality itself is an illusion, what lies beyond the veil?

Perhaps the greatest lesson of the Gnostic Gospels is this: *no external force can grant you truth. It is yours to find, yours to remember, and yours to reclaim.*

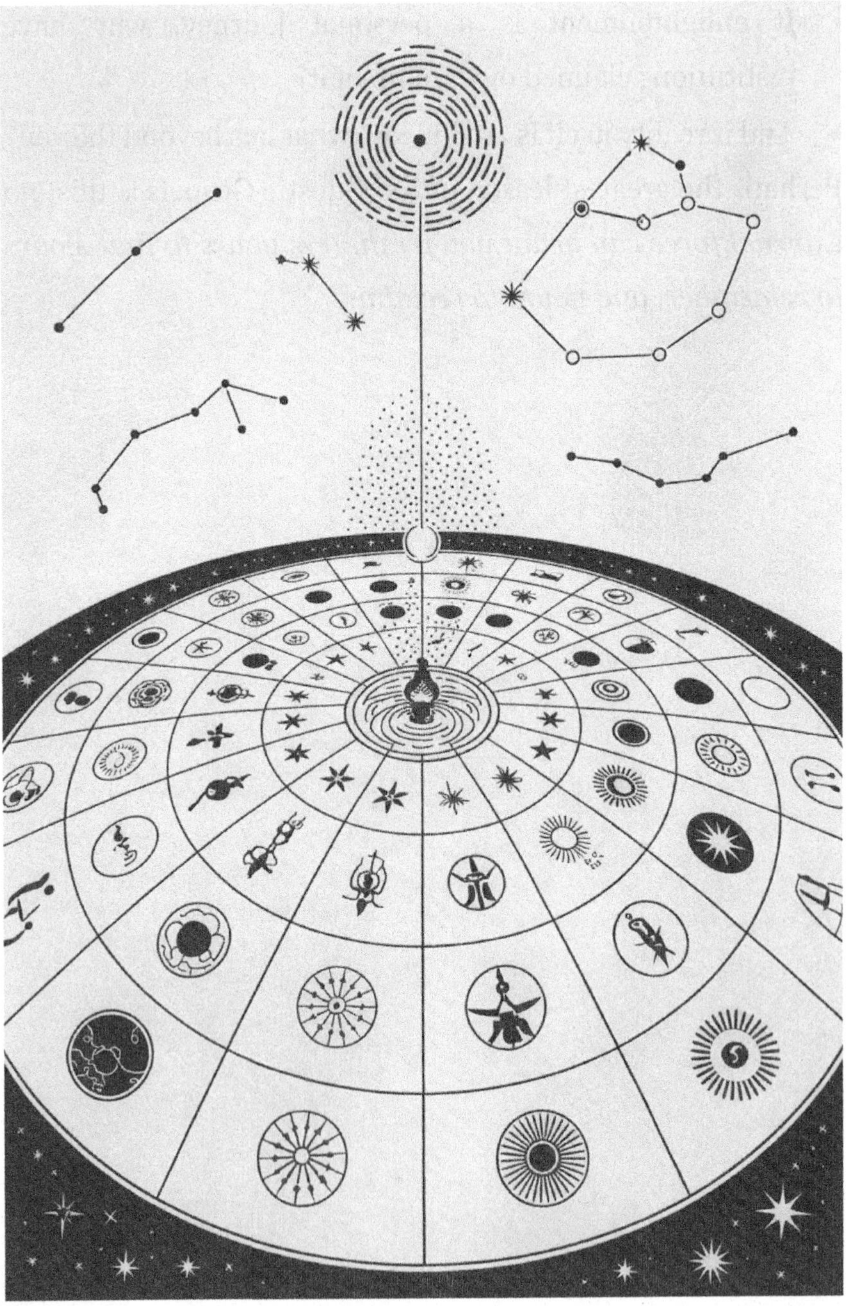

9. Pre-Columbian civilizations, like the *Maya*, measured time in great cycles, creating calendars that synchronized with cosmic movements in ways modern science is only beginning to understand.

Long before modern astronomers mapped the heavens, before mechanical clocks dictated the rhythm of human life, the ancient Maya had already unlocked *the deeper mechanics of time itself.* Unlike our linear perception of time, their understanding was cyclical—*an eternal dance of cosmic rhythms, celestial alignments, and the unfolding of great ages.* Their calendars were not just methods of counting days; they were *keys to the structure of reality itself.*

Where did this knowledge come from? And why does it align so precisely with astronomical cycles that modern science has only recently begun to understand?

The Maya, along with other pre-Columbian civilizations, did not measure time as a straight path from past to future. Instead, they viewed it as *a series of repeating cycles*, each with its own unique energy, each influencing the consciousness of those who lived within it. They developed multiple interwoven calendars, each serving a different purpose, yet all synchronized with celestial events.

The most famous of these was the *Long Count Calendar*, which did not simply track years, but vast epochs of human history—*Great Cycles* lasting 5,125 years. It was this calendar that sparked global attention when its last recorded cycle ended on December 21, 2012. While mainstream media sensationalized this as a prophecy of the "end of the world," the Maya themselves saw it as nothing more than *the closing of one age and the beginning of another.*

But how did they develop such an advanced system? Their calculations were so precise that they measured the solar year more accurately than the Gregorian calendar we use today. They tracked the movements of Venus with a margin of error so small that even modern instruments struggle to improve upon it. They understood the concept of *precession*—the slow wobble of Earth's axis that takes nearly 26,000 years to complete—something that ancient civilizations supposedly should not have been able to detect.

Where did this knowledge originate?

The Maya spoke of gods and sky-beings who *taught them the secrets of time.* Their legends tell of *Quetzalcoatl*—a serpent deity associated with wisdom, astronomy, and the cycles of civilization. Similar myths appear across pre-Columbian cultures, hinting at *a lost lineage of knowledge* that predates known history.

If the Maya were simply early mathematicians, their precision alone would be astonishing. But there is something deeper at play—an awareness of *the interconnectedness between time, consciousness, and cosmic forces.* Their calendar was not just a tool for tracking days; it was a means of aligning human civilization with the rhythm of the universe itself.

They believed that different time periods carried different energetic qualities. Some ages were *creative and expansive*, others were *destructive and chaotic*. Their calendar system allowed them to *predict cycles of growth, decline, and transformation*—not in a superstitious way, but through *an understanding of how cosmic forces influence human events.* This concept closely mirrors ideas found in other ancient traditions. The Hindu *Yugas* describe great cosmic ages of humanity, cycling through times of enlightenment and darkness. The Egyptian *Zep Tepi* refers to a lost golden age of the gods, before a great catastrophe reset civilization. Even modern science acknowledges cycles of mass extinctions and planetary changes that seem to align with *larger cosmic rhythms*.

Could it be that the Maya were tapping into *a universal knowledge*, one that was once understood by civilizations long before recorded history?

The structures they left behind suggest as much. The pyramid of *El Castillo* in Chichén Itzá is not just an architectural marvel—it is a calendar in stone. During the equinoxes, a serpent-shaped shadow slithers down the steps of the pyramid, marking the shift in celestial energies. The Temple of the Sun at Teotihuacan aligns perfectly with key solar events, as if it were built *not just to honor the sun, but to interact with its cycles.*

Why were they so obsessed with cosmic alignment? And why do their monuments resonate with mathematical constants that govern both *astronomical mechanics and human consciousness*?

Some researchers believe that the Maya, like other ancient civilizations, inherited their knowledge from a forgotten source—*a lost civilization, or perhaps something even more mysterious*. The similarities between their understanding of time and that of other ancient cultures suggest a shared origin, a once-unified knowledge that was later fragmented across the world.

If this is true, then what else did they know?

Their texts, carved into stone and preserved in secret codices, may hold further revelations. But much of their written knowledge was destroyed. The Spanish Conquistadors, seeing their wisdom as a threat to religious dominance, burned thousands of sacred books, erasing generations of astronomical observations and metaphysical insights.

Yet, despite this destruction, the echoes of their knowledge persist. Modern science is only now beginning to confirm what the Maya understood centuries ago—that *time is not just a measurement, but a force, a current, an ever-unfolding cosmic pattern that shapes the reality we perceive.*

If their calendars were so accurate, so advanced, and so deeply connected to cosmic rhythms, then we must ask:

What did they see that we have forgotten?

And are we, too, standing on the threshold of a new cycle—one that, like the Maya believed, will transform our understanding of the universe itself?

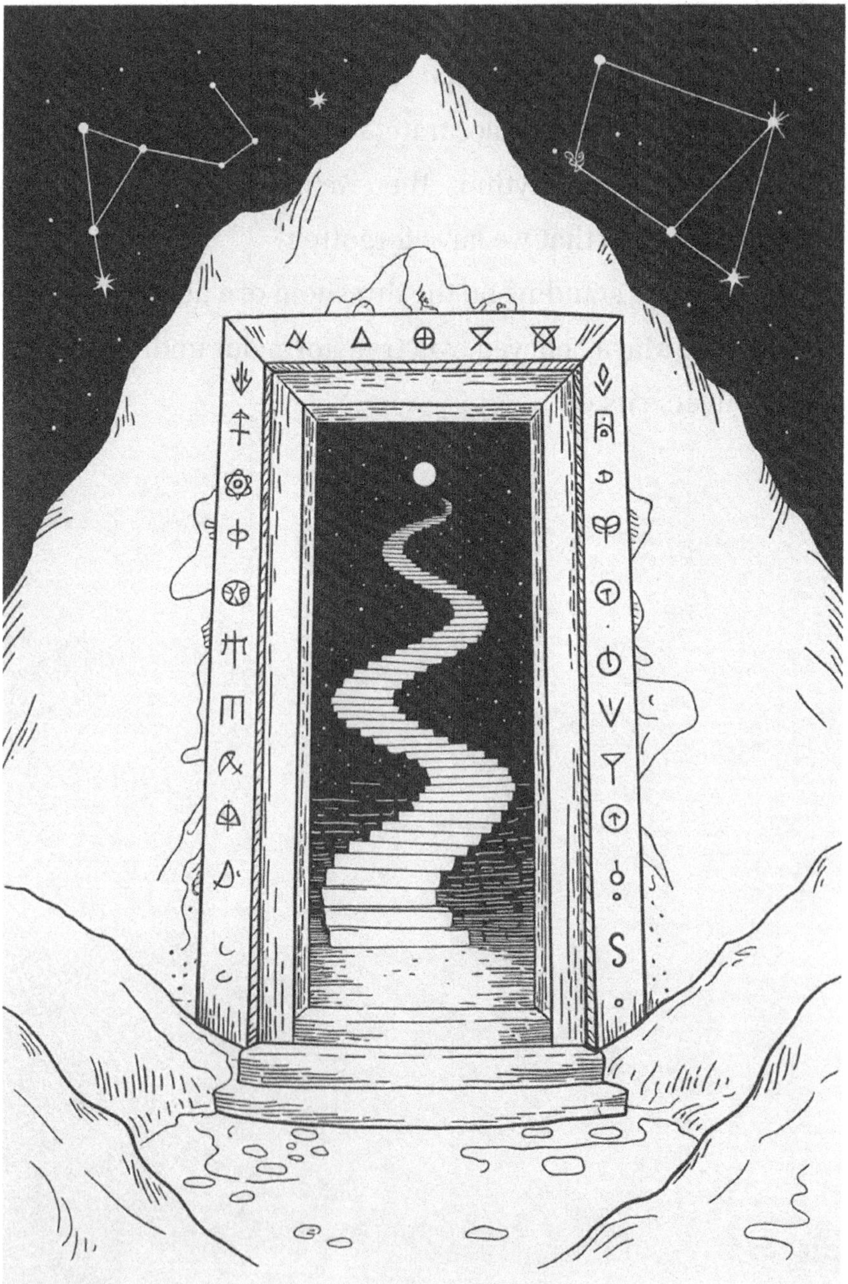

10. The *Nazca Lines,* massive geoglyphs visible only from above, could have been *star maps, ritual symbols, or messages meant for higher entities.*

The vast, desolate plains of the Peruvian desert hold a mystery so grand that it can only be fully grasped from the sky. The Nazca Lines—colossal geoglyphs carved into the earth—depict intricate geometric patterns, spirals, animals, and lines stretching for miles with no apparent destination. They were made by a civilization that had no aerial technology, yet they can only be seen in their entirety from above. Who were they meant for?

The Nazca civilization flourished between 500 BCE and 500 CE, a time when most societies relied on rudimentary tools and localized knowledge. Yet, they created one of the largest and most inexplicable works of art on the planet. Their methods, while seemingly simple—removing the reddish-brown iron oxide pebbles to expose the lighter-colored ground beneath—were executed with extraordinary precision. But why would they design something so massive if they had no means of seeing it?

Some believe the Nazca Lines were celestial maps, aligning with constellations, planetary movements, and solstices.

Ancient civilizations across the world built monuments in alignment with the heavens. The Egyptians with Orion's Belt, the Maya with Venus, the builders of Stonehenge with the solstices. If the Nazca followed this same cosmic principle, were they mapping the stars onto the earth? As Hermes Trismegistus said, *"As above, so below."* If this principle guided the architects of the Great Pyramid, did it also guide the Nazca?

The presence of animals among the glyphs suggests something more than just an astronomical calendar. The hummingbird, the spider, the monkey—each animal holds spiritual significance. In many ancient traditions, animals were messengers between worlds, linking humans with the divine. Were these glyphs offerings, symbols meant to invoke protection, or were they paths of energy meant to be followed in ritual? Some researchers propose that the Nazca walked along these lines in sacred ceremonies, tracing their paths in prayers to the gods or higher forces. Fragments of pottery and other ritual objects found near the glyphs suggest that they were places of worship.

Yet there is another, more provocative theory. The sheer scale of the lines, the perfect symmetry, the long, ruler-straight paths—these are unlike anything else found in ancient art. Some of these lines stretch over ten miles without deviation. From the ground, they seem random, almost meaningless.

From the air, they take form. If they were meant to be seen from the sky, who were they meant for?

Ancient texts across cultures describe beings who arrived from above, descending in fiery chariots, teaching humanity secrets of civilization. The Book of Ezekiel speaks of a vision in which a great whirlwind appears from the heavens, revealing a celestial chariot with wheels full of eyes, moving in ways unnatural to earthly laws. Hindu scriptures describe vimanas, flying crafts used by gods. The Maya recorded the descent of Quetzalcoatl, the feathered serpent, as a bringer of wisdom from the sky.

Did the Nazca people witness something similar? Were they calling out to something—or someone—beyond this world? Some believe the long straight lines resemble landing strips, though this idea is dismissed by mainstream archaeology. Yet, in an age where the Nazca had no means of seeing their own work from above, why design paths that stretch endlessly, as if pointing toward the heavens?

Even if the answer is not extraterrestrial, the mystery deepens when considering the unique properties of the Nazca desert. The region contains high levels of iron oxide, and some lines pass through areas of unusual magnetic activity. Ancient cultures across the world recognized ley lines—energetic pathways within the earth. Could the Nazca Lines be an ancient attempt to harness or direct these unseen forces?

Much of the Nazca civilization's knowledge was lost when the Spanish conquest brought destruction to the indigenous peoples of the Andes. Like the Maya, like the Gnostics, like the countless other cultures whose wisdom threatened the structures of power, their legacy was erased. What remains is not written texts or monuments of stone, but messages carved into the very fabric of the earth itself.

Were they maps of the stars, sacred ritual paths, or signals meant for something beyond our comprehension? Or do they represent a universal truth about the connection between the earth, the cosmos, and the unseen forces that shape reality?

Perhaps the desert still holds its secrets. Perhaps we are only beginning to remember what was once known.

Phase 2 – The Veil: Destruction, Manipulation, and the Loss of Truths

"The greatest enemy of knowledge is not ignorance, it is the illusion of knowledge."

— Stephen Hawking

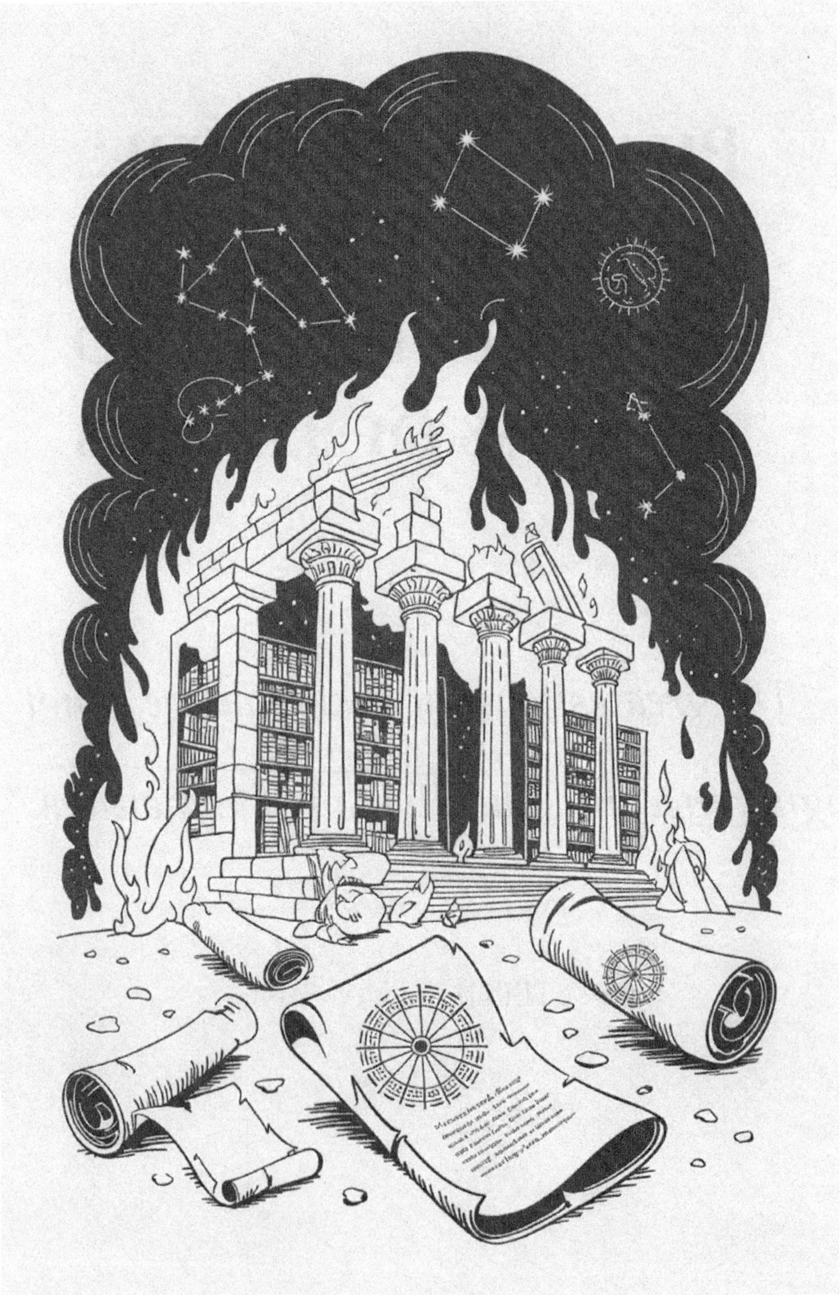

11. The *Library of Alexandria*, the greatest repository of ancient knowledge, was *burned multiple times*, wiping out scientific and esoteric texts that could have rewritten history

The Library of Alexandria was more than a collection of texts. It was a sanctuary of knowledge, a beacon of enlightenment where the greatest minds of the ancient world gathered to explore the mysteries of existence. Mathematics, astronomy, medicine, engineering—every known discipline was studied within its walls. But beyond these sciences, there were whispers of something more. Hidden within its vast archives, some believe, were texts that contained truths far older than recorded history, insights into lost civilizations, forbidden sciences, and knowledge that could have rewritten the story of humanity.

Then, it was gone.

Destroyed in a series of fires and conflicts, the loss of the Library of Alexandria remains one of history's greatest tragedies. What knowledge was lost forever? How different would our world be if those texts had survived? And perhaps the most unsettling question of all—was its destruction merely a tragic accident, or was it intentional?

The official story tells of multiple fires, each chipping away at the Library's vast collection. Julius Caesar's siege of Alexandria in 48 BCE is often cited as the first major destruction. Later, Emperor Aurelian's battles in the city may have caused further damage. Religious purges under Theophilus and subsequent conquests supposedly erased what remained. But how could a single fire—or even multiple fires—completely obliterate a collection that spanned continents and centuries? Was this simply an unfortunate consequence of war, or was it part of a larger effort to erase something that was never meant to be found again?

The rulers of Alexandria sought knowledge at any cost. Ships arriving at the city's port were searched, and any scrolls discovered were copied before the originals were returned—if they were returned at all. The Library was not just a repository; it was an ever-growing organism, absorbing wisdom from Egypt, Greece, Mesopotamia, India, and beyond. Within its halls, scholars debated not just the mechanics of the physical world but the very fabric of reality itself.

What if the Library contained knowledge that threatened the existing order?

There are accounts suggesting that some texts went far beyond conventional sciences. Some believe that within the lost scrolls were writings on alchemy, energy manipulation, and the fundamental nature of consciousness. Others speculate that the Library housed remnants of an even older civilization, possibly linked to Atlantis or other lost worlds, preserving records of technology and wisdom far beyond what should have existed at the time.

Could it be that the destruction of the Library was not a random tragedy, but a deliberate act of suppression?

Throughout history, knowledge has always been the first casualty of control. When ideas challenge the established power structures, they are silenced. When discoveries threaten to shift the balance of authority, they disappear. The destruction of the Library was not just the burning of books—it was the erasure of an entire branch of human evolution, a path we will never know.

And yet, fragments of that knowledge have survived. Scattered references to lost sciences and forgotten wisdom appear in ancient texts from different cultures. Concepts that should not have existed for centuries—mathematical principles, astronomical calculations, even medical procedures—are hinted at in civilizations that had no known means of discovering them.

Was this knowledge truly lost, or was it hidden? If some of it survived, where is it now?

If the Library had endured, how would our world look today? Would we have advanced centuries ahead of our time? Would we have understood the deeper nature of the universe, of consciousness, of reality itself?

Or did someone ensure that we never would?

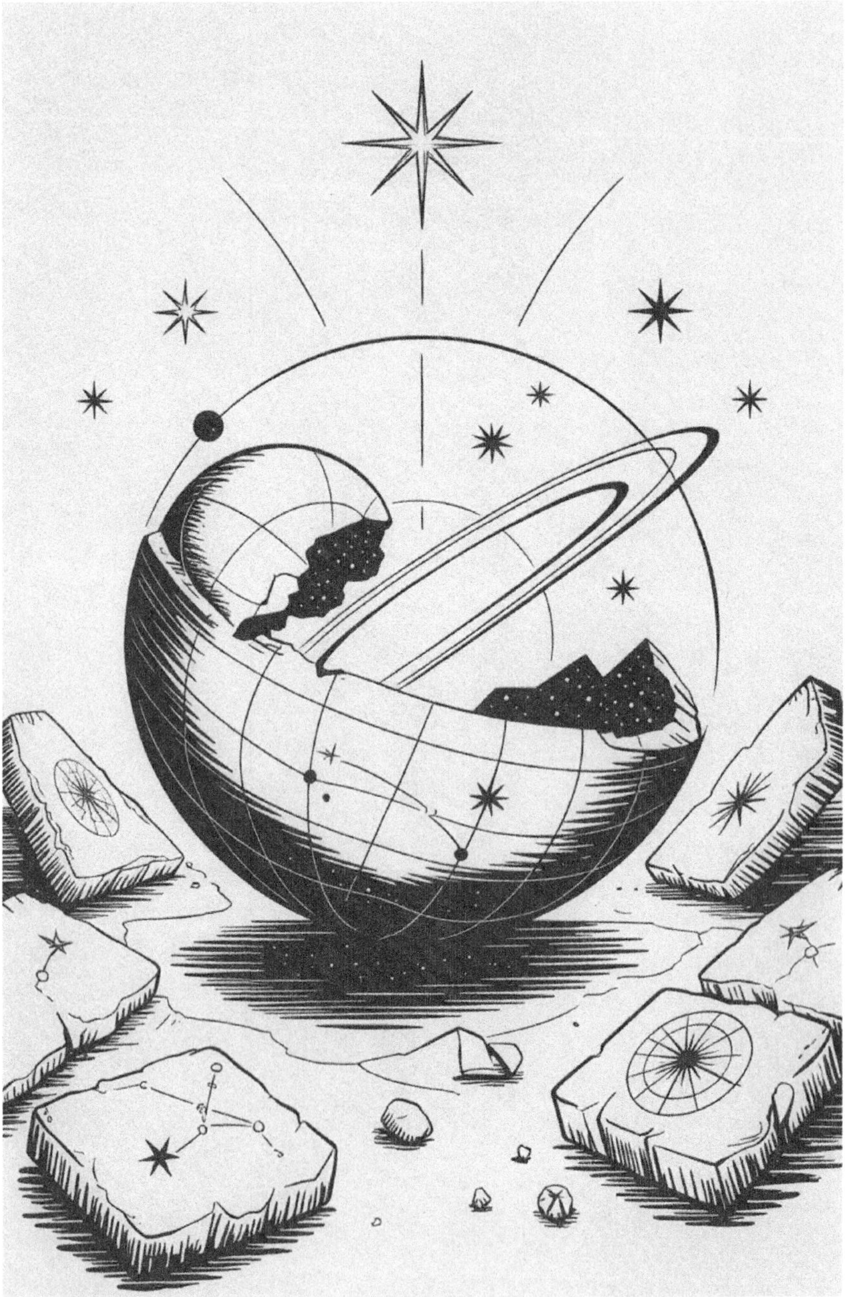

12. *Giordano Bruno* was executed in 1600 for declaring that the universe was infinite and that higher laws existed beyond religious dogma.

Giordano Bruno was not merely a philosopher or a scientist. He was a visionary, a man who saw beyond the boundaries imposed by his time, daring to challenge the rigid doctrines that governed thought and belief. At the dawn of the 17th century, when the universe was still perceived as a finite structure centered around the Earth, Bruno spoke of something far more unsettling. He proclaimed that the cosmos was infinite, that countless worlds existed beyond our own, and that the true nature of reality was governed by laws beyond the reach of religious institutions.

For this, he was condemned.

On February 17, 1600, in the heart of Rome, Giordano Bruno was led to the Campo de' Fiori. He had been imprisoned for years, interrogated, and pressured to recant his views. He refused. The inquisitors declared him a heretic, and as the flames consumed him, so too did centuries of accumulated wisdom that he carried within him. But was his execution merely about religious defiance, or was there something deeper at stake?

Bruno's ideas were dangerous not only because they contradicted the teachings of the Church but because they threatened the very structure of power. The belief in an infinite universe shattered the notion of a world designed solely for humankind. If the stars were not just distant lights but suns with their own planetary systems, what did that imply? If life could exist elsewhere, what did that say about humanity's supposed divine uniqueness? If higher laws existed beyond religious dogma, what need was there for institutions that claimed to hold exclusive access to truth?

His execution was not just the silencing of a man but the suppression of a radical shift in consciousness. The idea of an infinite universe was too much for the authorities to allow. Knowledge had to be controlled, shaped, and contained within the framework of accepted belief. Anything that threatened to expand the human mind beyond those constraints was seen as a direct challenge to power.

Yet, despite their efforts, his ideas could not be burned away. Bruno's vision foreshadowed discoveries that would emerge centuries later. The vastness of space, the existence of exoplanets, the understanding that the cosmos is not a static creation but an ever-expanding mystery—these revelations align more with his heretical views than with the doctrines that sought to erase him. What if his ideas had been embraced instead of condemned? What scientific advancements were delayed because of the fear his knowledge instilled?

More than four hundred years later, his words still resonate. He was not merely a man ahead of his time—he was a man from a different paradigm altogether, one that the world was not ready for. But now, in an age where science is only beginning to grasp the complexities of the universe, his vision seems less like a heresy and more like a truth that was never meant to be forgotten.

Perhaps, in the grand cycle of knowledge and suppression, there are always those who see too much, who understand too soon. And perhaps, despite their persecution, their ideas never truly die.

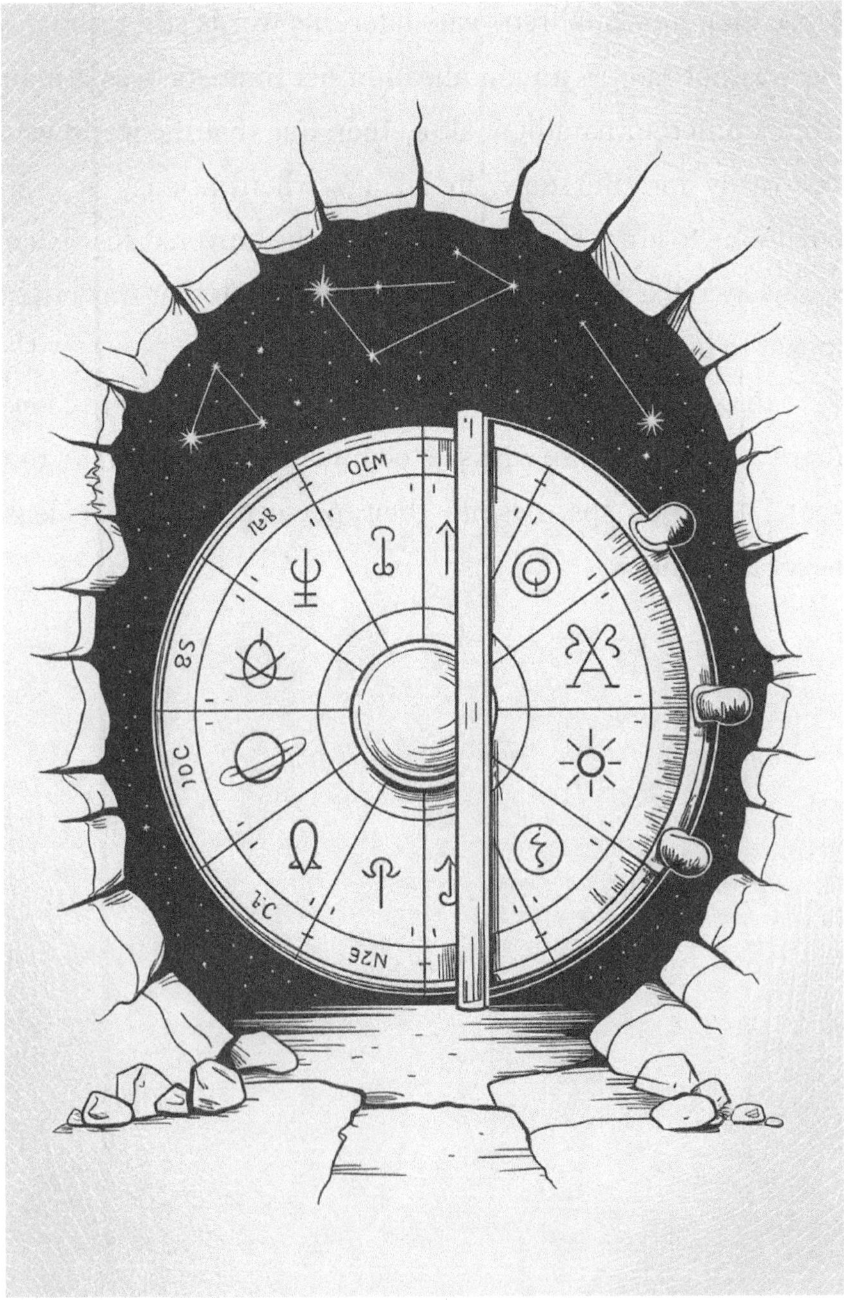

13. The *Knights Templar*, guardians of lost spiritual knowledge, were accused of heresy and exterminated—not just for their power, but for what they knew.

The Knights Templar were more than warriors. They were scholars, mystics, and guardians of knowledge that stretched beyond the reach of the medieval Church. Officially, they were a monastic military order, sworn to protect Christian pilgrims in the Holy Land. Unofficially, they became something far greater—custodians of ancient wisdom, keepers of secrets that had the potential to reshape the very foundations of religious and political power.

For nearly two centuries, the Templars grew in influence. Their network extended across Europe and the Middle East. They amassed wealth, built fortresses, and developed an independent financial system that rivaled the power of monarchs. But it was not their riches that sealed their fate. It was what they knew.

The official narrative tells us that on Friday, October 13, 1307, King Philip IV of France ordered the mass arrest of the Templars, accusing them of heresy, blasphemy, and occult practices. Under torture, some confessed to worshipping strange idols, performing secretive rituals, and possessing knowledge forbidden by the Church. Many of these confessions were later recanted, but it did not matter. The verdict had already been decided. The order was dissolved, its leaders burned at the stake, and its surviving members either absorbed into other groups or hunted into obscurity.

But the question remains—was this truly about heresy, or was it about something else?

The Templars had spent years in the Holy Land, where they came into contact with Islamic scholars, Sufi mystics, and remnants of esoteric traditions older than Christianity itself. Some believe they discovered hidden truths buried beneath the ruins of Jerusalem, possibly in the Temple of Solomon—the very place from which they derived their name. Did they uncover lost scriptures, sacred relics, or knowledge that contradicted the teachings of the Church?

Rumors persist that the Templars held texts related to early Gnostic Christianity, revealing a version of Christ's teachings that diverged from official doctrine. Others claim they possessed fragments of ancient wisdom from Egypt or Babylon, records of civilizations that understood the nature of energy, consciousness, and the structure of reality in ways modern science is only beginning to grasp. If they had access to such knowledge, it would have made them not only powerful but dangerous to those who sought to control belief and knowledge.

King Philip IV was deeply in debt to the Templars. By orchestrating their downfall, he not only erased his financial obligations but also secured favor with the Church. Yet, financial motives alone do not explain the relentless persecution of the order. It was not enough to disband them; their history had to be rewritten, their legacy erased, their teachings suppressed.

Even in death, their influence did not disappear. The remnants of the Templars did not simply vanish. Some believe they took their knowledge underground, forming the foundations of later secret societies. Others suggest that their wisdom was scattered, hidden in symbols and allegories, waiting for those with the eyes to see and the mind to understand.

Were the Templars truly guilty of the heresies they were accused of, or was their real crime something far greater—possessing truths that those in power could not allow to be known?

What if their lost knowledge still lingers, buried in forgotten texts, encoded in ancient structures, concealed beneath layers of deception?

Perhaps the real secret of the Templars was not what they believed, but what they refused to forget.

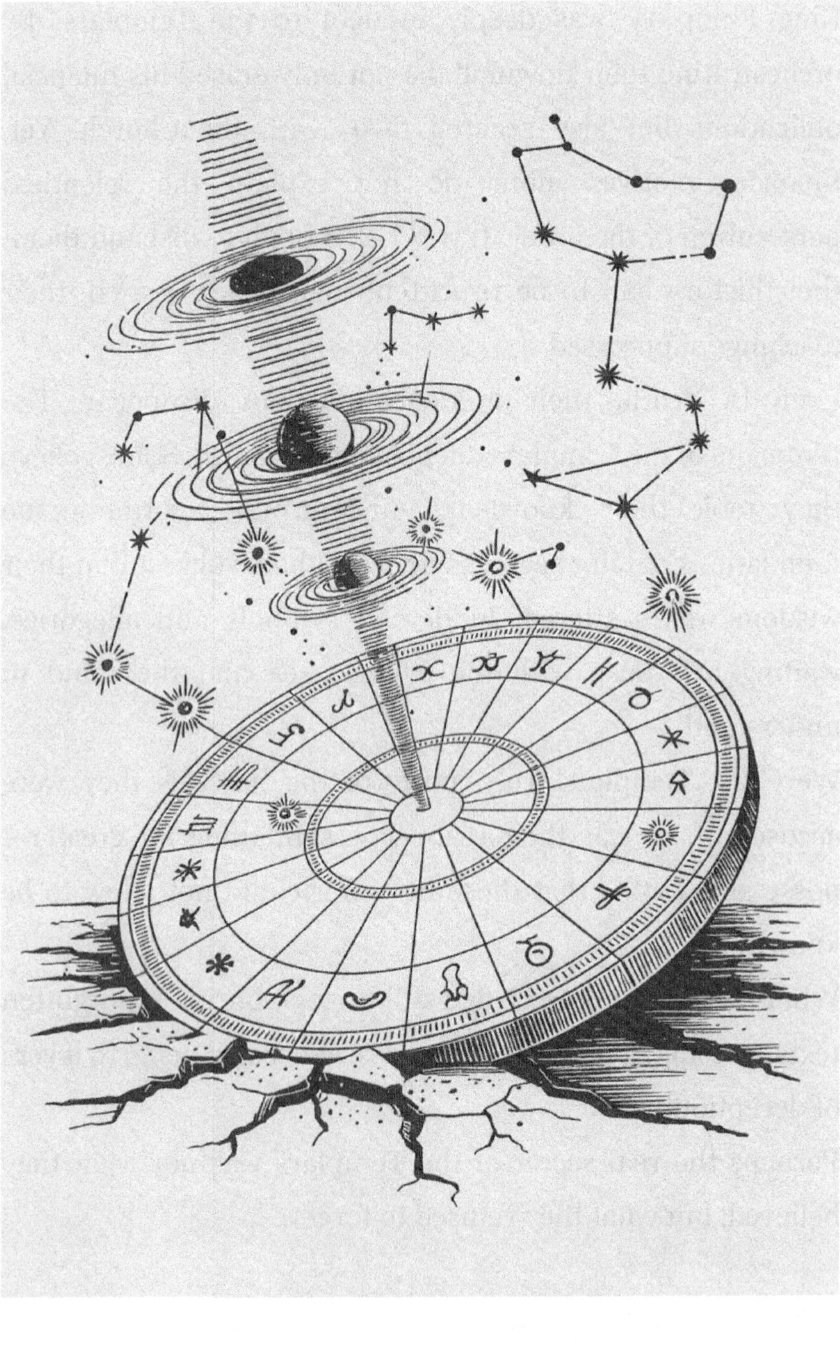

14. Symbols once associated with divine wisdom were *demonized*: the pentagram, once a symbol of protection, became a mark of the forbidden

The power of symbols lies in their ability to communicate truths that words cannot contain. Across cultures and civilizations, they have been used to convey *divine wisdom*, to encode knowledge, and to bridge the gap between the seen and the unseen. But symbols are not static. Their meanings shift, sometimes naturally, but more often by design. When those in power seek to control knowledge, they do not merely suppress ideas—they *corrupt their meaning*, turning once-sacred emblems into marks of fear and condemnation.

Few symbols illustrate this transformation more than the pentagram.

For thousands of years, the pentagram stood as a representation of harmony, balance, and protection. It was a mathematical perfection, a reflection of the *divine order* embedded in nature. Its five points corresponded to the *five elements*—earth, air, fire, water, and ether—the very forces that shape reality. It was a symbol carried by scholars, mystics, and those who sought understanding beyond the limits of the material world. And then, it was rewritten.

The origins of the pentagram trace back to the earliest known civilizations. In Mesopotamia, the Sumerians inscribed it on clay tablets as a symbol of power and cosmic balance. To the Babylonians, it was a *protective sigil*, often used in rituals to ward off evil. Later, the Greeks saw the pentagram not just as a sacred shape but as a mathematical code. The Pythagoreans, a secretive order of philosophers and mathematicians, regarded it as a representation of the *Golden Ratio*, the mysterious proportion that appears throughout nature, from the spirals of galaxies to the patterns in shells and flowers. They saw the pentagram as a *key to understanding reality itself*, a reflection of an underlying intelligence in the universe. This sacred geometry was carried into *esoteric traditions* across the world. In Egyptian temples, it appeared in hieroglyphic inscriptions associated with the balance between spirit and matter. In early Christianity, it was sometimes used to represent the *five wounds of Christ*, a symbol of divine sacrifice and redemption. In medieval Europe, it was a common sign of *protection*, worn by knights and carved into doorways to ward off malevolent forces. At its core, the pentagram was a *symbol of enlightenment*, a tool for those who sought to uncover hidden truths. But knowledge that empowers is also knowledge that threatens.

As centralized religious institutions gained power, they became the sole arbiters of truth. Independent thought, mystical exploration, and alternative spiritual practices were seen as dangerous. The same symbols that once guided seekers of wisdom were now *branded as heretical*. The pentagram, once a sign of divine harmony, became associated with *witchcraft, heresy, and forbidden knowledge*. The medieval Church began linking it to secret societies, alchemical practices, and esoteric teachings that operated outside their control. The Inquisition saw it as a mark of rebellion, an emblem carried by those who defied established doctrine.

By the time of the witch trials, the pentagram had been fully transformed. It was no longer a sign of *spiritual balance* but a symbol of *sorcery*. Those accused of practicing forbidden arts were said to draw pentagrams on the ground, invoking powers that defied the will of the Church. Entire traditions of ancient knowledge—alchemy, astrology, sacred geometry— were cast into the shadows, labeled as the work of dark forces. The narrative of the pentagram was rewritten, not because its meaning had changed, but because its original purpose *threatened the structures of power*.

One of the most profound shifts in the pentagram's meaning occurred in the 19th and 20th centuries. It was during this period that the idea of the *inverted pentagram* as a symbol of darkness and inversion of natural order became widely popularized. Occultists such as Eliphas Levi and later Aleister Crowley reinterpreted the pentagram, associating its upright position with *spirit over matter*, while its reversed form became a representation of *matter dominating spirit*.

This new interpretation fueled modern fears, reinforcing the belief that the pentagram—especially when inverted—was a *symbol of the forbidden*, tied to secretive organizations, black magic, and subversive knowledge. By the time popular culture adopted these associations, the transformation was complete. What had once been a *universal symbol of wisdom* was now seen almost exclusively as a mark of the occult. Movies, books, and media reinforced its connection to the sinister and the supernatural, ensuring that its true origins were buried under centuries of fear and misunderstanding.

But symbols are powerful because their meaning can never be fully erased. Even as the pentagram was demonized, it continued to appear—hidden in architecture, embedded in sacred sites, quietly preserved in esoteric traditions.

Today, there is a resurgence of interest in *restoring its original meaning*. Scholars, historians, and spiritual seekers are once again recognizing the pentagram as a *symbol of knowledge, balance, and the interconnected forces of nature*. It has re-emerged in *alchemy, sacred geometry, and spiritual philosophies*, not as a mark of darkness, but as a reminder of lost wisdom.

The question remains—why was it altered in the first place?

If symbols hold power, then controlling their meaning controls how people *perceive reality*. By distorting the pentagram's significance, those in power reshaped not just a single image, but the way people view *knowledge, mysticism, and the pursuit of truth.*

How many other symbols have been rewritten? How many pieces of wisdom have been hidden behind layers of fear and deception?

Perhaps the real lesson of the pentagram is not in what it became, but in *what it was meant to reveal.*

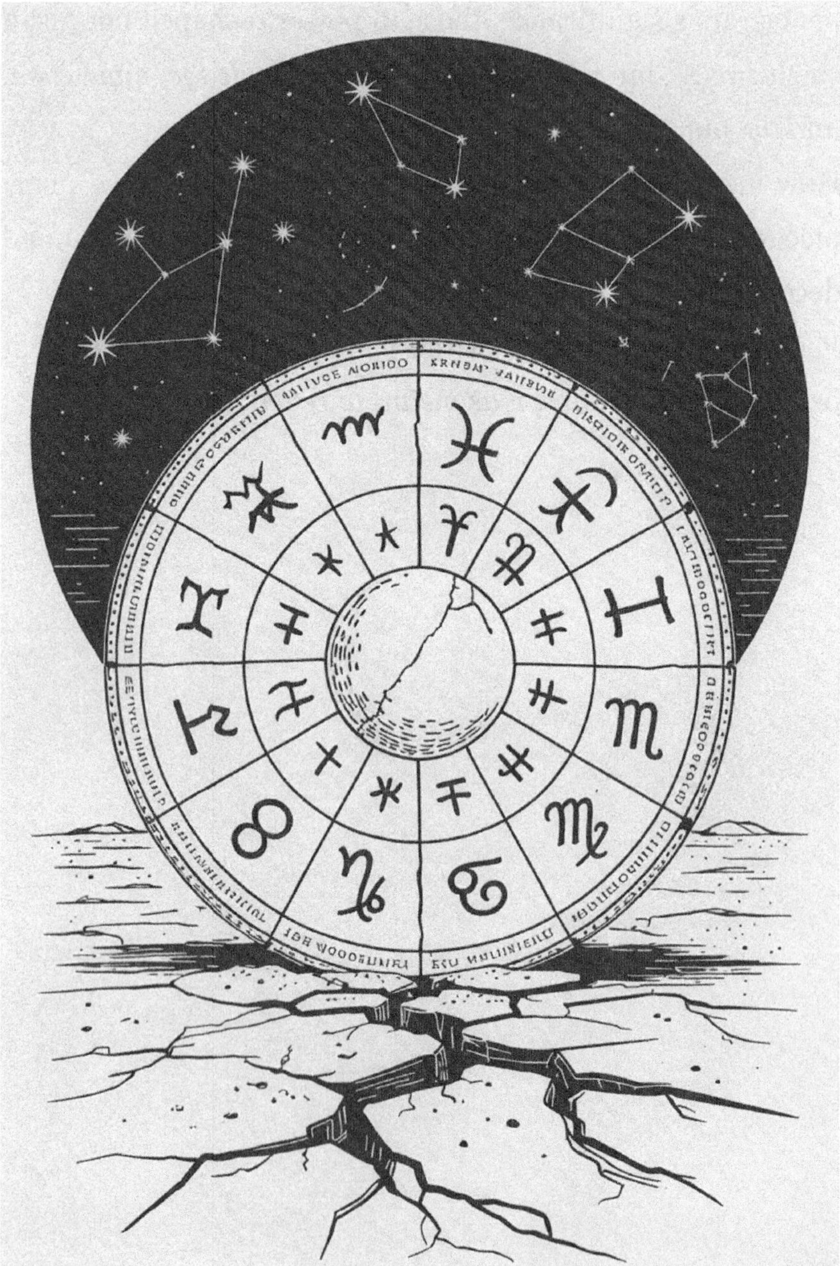

15. The *Council of Nicaea* (325 AD) reshaped religious history, deciding which scriptures would be included in the Bible, erasing *Gnosticism, reincarnation, and teachings on spiritual autonomy.*

The Council of Nicaea, convened in 325 AD by Emperor Constantine, was far more than a theological gathering. It was a turning point in religious history, a moment where the narrative of Christianity was reshaped, doctrines were decided, and entire streams of thought were erased from mainstream acceptance. Though often presented as a noble attempt to unify Christian belief, the reality is far more complex. The council did not merely define doctrine—it established what could and could not be considered divine truth. In doing so, it effectively silenced alternative perspectives, eliminating ideas that had once been integral to early Christian thought.

Before the council, Christianity was not a monolithic faith. It was a vast and diverse movement, with various sects, each holding different beliefs about the nature of Christ, the structure of the universe, and the path to salvation. Some groups, particularly the Gnostics, taught that spiritual enlightenment came from direct knowledge rather than blind faith. They believed that the material world was an illusion, a prison crafted by a false creator, and that salvation came from awakening to the divine spark within. Their teachings included reincarnation, the idea that souls would continue to return to the physical plane until they achieved true knowledge and liberation.

But such ideas posed a problem for the emerging church hierarchy. If salvation came from inner wisdom, what need was there for priests, bishops, or institutional authority? If individuals could find the divine within themselves, why would they need an external structure to dictate the terms of their faith? The teachings of Gnosticism, along with other esoteric interpretations of Christianity, were a direct challenge to the power of the church. And so, when the Council of Nicaea was convened, these ideas were not debated—they were erased.

The primary purpose of the council was to settle the question of Christ's divinity. At the time, there was no single, universally accepted doctrine regarding the nature of Jesus. Some groups, following the teachings of Arius, argued that Christ was created by God, a being of immense power but not equal to the Father. Others insisted on the concept of the Trinity, in which Christ was of the same divine essence as God. The debate was fierce, but ultimately, the council declared Arianism heretical and established the doctrine of the Trinity as the foundation of Christian belief. This decision would shape the course of Western religious thought for centuries to come.

But beyond theological disputes, the Council of Nicaea had another, equally significant function—it determined which texts would be included in what would eventually become the official Bible. Dozens of writings, once revered by early Christian communities, were dismissed, banned, or outright destroyed. Many of these excluded texts contained teachings that contradicted the authority of the institutional church. The Gospel of Thomas, for example, emphasized self-discovery and inner divinity rather than external worship. The Gospel of Mary suggested that divine wisdom was accessible to all, regardless of hierarchy or gender. These writings, along with numerous others, were deemed dangerous, and over time, they were suppressed, lost, or destroyed.

The removal of reincarnation from Christian doctrine was one of the most profound erasures. Early Christian texts contained references to the idea that souls return in different lifetimes to refine their understanding and work through karmic lessons. This belief was not foreign to the ancient world—many of the surrounding cultures, including the Greeks, Egyptians, and Hindus, held similar views. Even within Judaism, certain mystical traditions contained ideas of soul transmigration. Yet, at Nicaea and in subsequent councils, this belief was stripped from official doctrine. Why? Perhaps because a belief in reincarnation would have undermined the church's growing emphasis on salvation through adherence to dogma. If one had multiple lifetimes to achieve spiritual growth, the urgency to obey a religious institution in a single lifetime would be greatly diminished.

The elimination of alternative Christian teachings was not immediate. It took centuries of suppression, destruction of texts, and persecution of those who clung to forbidden beliefs. The Gnostic sects, once flourishing, were driven underground, their writings hidden in remote locations. It was not until the discovery of the Nag Hammadi library in 1945 that many of these lost texts resurfaced, revealing just how much had been removed from the official narrative.

The effects of the Council of Nicaea can still be felt today. The Bible, as most people know it, is not a complete record of early Christian thought—it is a curated selection, shaped by political and religious motivations. The doctrines that emerged from Nicaea became the foundation of Western religious thought, while alternative perspectives were buried, ridiculed, or forgotten.

But the question remains: what knowledge was lost? What spiritual insights were erased in favor of control? If the teachings of self-discovery, reincarnation, and direct access to the divine had remained, how differently would history have unfolded? Would humanity have been more spiritually autonomous, less reliant on external structures for salvation?

Would the deep wisdom of the ancients, preserved in esoteric traditions, have flourished rather than being forced into the shadows?

Perhaps the real legacy of Nicaea is not just in what it established, but in what it silenced. And as lost knowledge continues to resurface, perhaps it is time to revisit the past with open eyes, to question what we have been told, and to seek the truths that were meant to be forgotten.

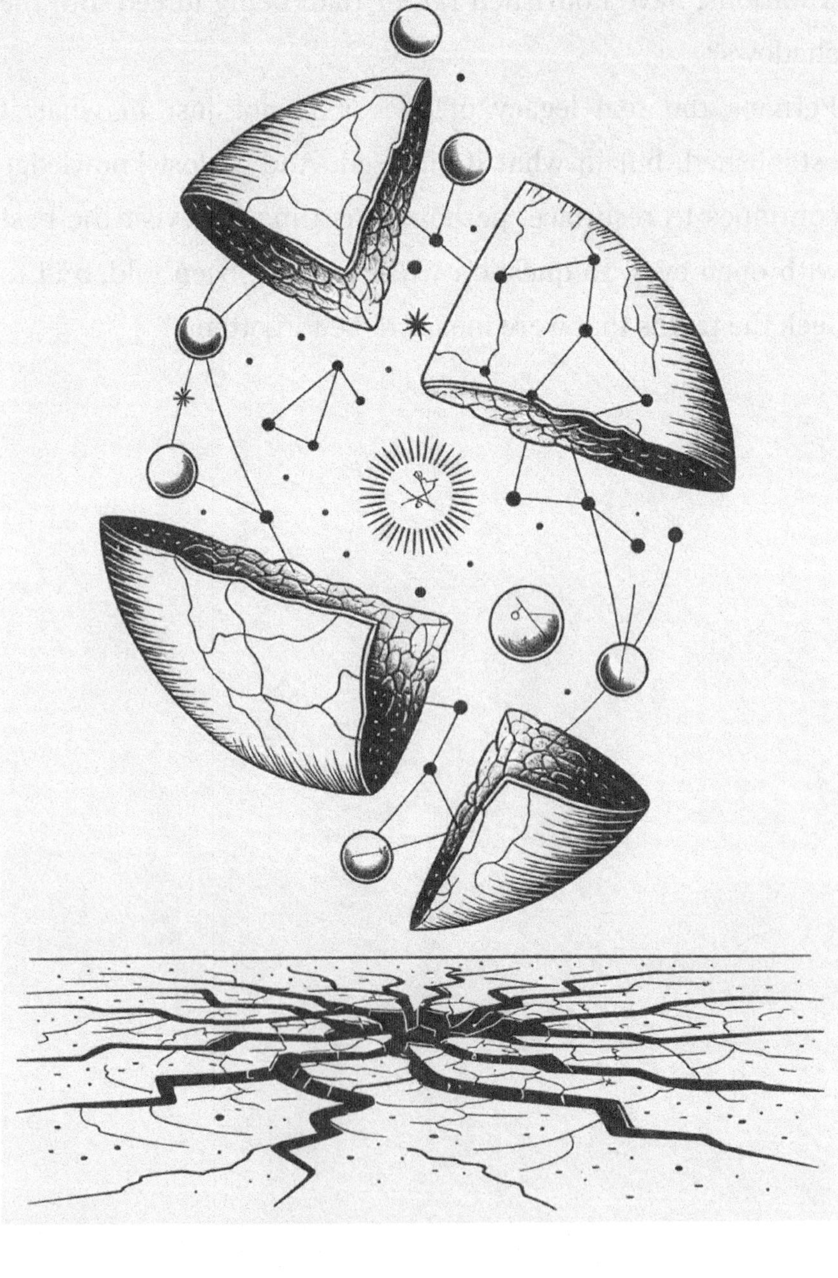

16. The *pineal gland,* called the *third eye* by the ancients, was dismissed as irrelevant by modern science—yet it is now known to produce *DMT, the "spirit molecule."*

For centuries, ancient traditions have spoken of an organ within the human body that acts as a gateway to higher consciousness, an internal link between the physical and the spiritual. They called it the third eye, the seat of the soul, the doorway to enlightenment. In modern anatomical terms, it is known as the pineal gland—a small, pea-shaped structure buried deep within the brain, precisely at its center. To the ancients, this was no ordinary gland. It was the key to perception beyond the five senses, a means of accessing higher dimensions of reality. Yet for much of recent history, science dismissed it as little more than a biological relic, a functionally irrelevant part of the brain with no significant purpose.

But as research into consciousness and neurochemistry has advanced, a startling revelation has emerged. The pineal gland is not only active, but it is also responsible for the production of one of the most mysterious compounds known to science: dimethyltryptamine, or DMT. Often referred to as the "spirit molecule," this naturally occurring substance is linked to profound, otherworldly experiences. Those who have encountered it describe visions of intricate, hyper-real landscapes, encounters with entities, and a sense of being transported beyond the limits of ordinary perception. The implications of this are staggering. Could it be that the third eye of ancient traditions was not merely symbolic, but a real, functional organ capable of unlocking hidden aspects of consciousness?

Ancient civilizations seemed to understand the significance of the pineal gland in ways that modern science is only beginning to grasp. In Hinduism, the third eye is represented by the ajna chakra, depicted as a point of divine vision located at the center of the forehead. Yogis and mystics have long practiced techniques to activate this energy center, believing that doing so grants access to higher states of awareness. The ancient Egyptians, too, placed great importance on this hidden organ. The Eye of Horus, one of their most sacred symbols, bears a striking resemblance to the anatomical structure of the pineal gland when viewed in cross-section. To them, it was the source of spiritual insight, a connection to the gods.

Western esoteric traditions echoed these beliefs. The philosopher René Descartes famously referred to the pineal gland as the "seat of the soul," suggesting that it was the primary interface between the body and the mind. For centuries, secret societies and mystical schools have sought methods to awaken the third eye, convinced that doing so would grant them access to deeper truths. Yet, despite these widespread ancient understandings, the modern scientific world dismissed such claims as superstition. The pineal gland was regarded as little more than a vestigial structure, a minor part of the endocrine system responsible only for regulating sleep cycles through the production of melatonin.

That assumption began to change when researchers discovered the presence of DMT within the pineal gland of mammals. DMT, a powerful psychoactive compound, induces experiences remarkably similar to descriptions of mystical states, near-death experiences, and even alien encounters. Some speculate that the pineal gland releases DMT during moments of extreme consciousness shifts—birth, death, deep meditation, or intense visionary states. If true, this would suggest that the pineal gland is not just another gland in the brain, but a biological mechanism designed to facilitate experiences beyond ordinary perception.

The question then arises: why was this knowledge forgotten? Why did modern science ignore or suppress interest in the pineal gland for so long? Some researchers propose that there has been a deliberate effort, conscious or otherwise, to keep humanity focused solely on the material world. If the pineal gland truly acts as an interface between the human mind and greater cosmic awareness, then understanding its function could disrupt the carefully maintained belief that consciousness is merely a byproduct of brain chemistry rather than something far more expansive.

One of the more controversial discussions surrounding the pineal gland concerns its calcification. Studies show that the pineal gland in many adults becomes hardened over time, accumulating calcium deposits that impair its function. Some suggest that this is exacerbated by environmental factors such as fluoride in drinking water, dietary habits, and modern lifestyle choices. Could it be that widespread calcification of the pineal gland is not merely a coincidence but an unintentional (or even intentional) suppression of higher perception? Those who believe in this theory argue that restoring pineal function—through detoxification, meditation, and specific dietary changes—can lead to heightened states of awareness, increased intuition, and deeper spiritual experiences.

While the mainstream medical community remains skeptical, independent researchers continue to explore the pineal gland's role in consciousness. Some experiments suggest that deep meditation techniques, breathing exercises, and even sound frequencies may stimulate pineal activity. Anecdotal reports from spiritual practitioners claim that activating the third eye leads to vivid inner visions, heightened perception, and even glimpses into other realms of existence.

This brings us back to the ancient traditions. Were the sages, mystics, and philosophers of the past right all along? Did they possess knowledge about human consciousness that was lost or ignored by modern society? If the pineal gland is indeed a gateway to higher awareness, then what else have we forgotten? More importantly, what happens if humanity collectively reawakens this dormant potential?

Perhaps the real secret of the third eye is not simply its ability to generate psychedelic visions, but its role in shifting perception entirely. If consciousness is not confined to the brain, if awareness extends beyond the limits of material existence, then the pineal gland may serve as the bridge between two worlds—the physical and the metaphysical.

If this is the case, then what does it mean for the future? Will science eventually validate what ancient wisdom has always known? Or will this knowledge remain on the fringes, acknowledged only by those willing to seek it out? The answer, like the pineal gland itself, remains hidden—waiting for those who are ready to see.

106

17. The *All-Seeing Eye,* now embedded in modern symbols of power, was originally an esoteric sign of *spiritual enlightenment* (the *Eye of Horus*).

The All-Seeing Eye is one of the most enigmatic and misunderstood symbols in human history. It appears in religious texts, esoteric traditions, ancient artwork, and modern institutions of power. For some, it represents divine wisdom, the ability to perceive beyond the material world. For others, it is a symbol of control, surveillance, and hidden authority. But long before it became associated with secret societies and government emblems, it was something entirely different. It was a symbol of enlightenment, a mark of spiritual awakening, a reminder that true vision is not limited to the physical eyes.

The origins of the All-Seeing Eye stretch back thousands of years. The ancient Egyptians knew it as the Eye of Horus, a powerful symbol of protection, insight, and higher perception. Unlike an ordinary human eye, the Eye of Horus was said to perceive the unseen, to grasp realities beyond the veil of illusion. It was often depicted on temple walls, tombs, and amulets, meant to safeguard those who journeyed through the afterlife. But the story of the Eye of Horus was not just about protection. It was about loss, destruction, and ultimately, restoration.

According to Egyptian mythology, Horus, the falcon-headed god, fought a great battle against Set, the god of chaos. In this struggle, Horus lost his eye, a symbolic event representing the fragmentation of divine wisdom. Yet the eye was later restored, not merely as a physical organ but as a source of deeper knowledge. This restoration symbolized the process of awakening, the journey from blindness to sight, from ignorance to true understanding. It was a reminder that even in destruction, wisdom could be reclaimed.

The concept of an all-seeing, omnipresent eye did not remain confined to Egypt. Similar symbols appeared across different cultures, each carrying variations of the same idea. In Hindu traditions, the third eye was described as a center of intuition, an inner vision that allowed one to perceive beyond the ordinary. In Christian iconography, the Eye of Providence appeared within a radiant triangle, representing divine omniscience, a force that observes all things. In esoteric traditions, the eye was linked to enlightenment, representing the ability to see beyond deception, to recognize hidden truths.

Yet, despite its spiritual origins, the symbol of the All-Seeing Eye underwent a dramatic transformation. As centralized power structures took hold of ancient knowledge, the meaning of these symbols shifted. What was once a representation of inner wisdom and personal enlightenment became a mark of external control.

The most famous modern depiction of the All-Seeing Eye is found on the United States dollar bill, encased within a pyramid. This placement has fueled endless speculation. Some believe it is a tribute to the wisdom of ancient civilizations, a recognition of lost knowledge carried forward. Others see it as a declaration of dominance, an assertion that power is held by a hidden elite. Below the eye, the Latin phrase novus ordo seclorum translates to new order of the ages, a phrase that only deepens the mystery.

The Freemasons also adopted the All-Seeing Eye, referring to it as the Great Architect of the Universe. In this interpretation, it symbolized a guiding intelligence, a force that shaped reality itself. Yet, as secret societies became the subject of speculation and fear, the symbol too became tainted by suspicion. The idea of an all-seeing, ever-present watcher shifted from one of spiritual insight to one of control, surveillance, and hidden authority.

But was this transformation accidental, or was it intentional? Throughout history, symbols have been rewritten, their meanings reshaped to serve those who wield power. By altering the perception of a symbol, those in control reshape the way people understand their own reality. What was once a tool for liberation becomes a mark of oppression. What was once an invitation to seek knowledge becomes a warning to remain obedient.

Yet, despite these distortions, the original essence of the All-Seeing Eye has never truly disappeared. Even today, many recognize it as a symbol of awareness, of breaking through illusion, of seeing beyond the surface. It serves as a reminder that true vision is not about physical sight, but about perception, about recognizing what lies beneath the narratives presented to us.

If the Eye of Horus was meant to signify wisdom and restoration, then perhaps its presence in modern structures is not merely a sign of control, but also a hidden clue. A message left in plain sight, waiting for those who are willing to see it for what it truly is.

What if the greatest deception was not the existence of an all-seeing presence, but the conditioning that taught us to fear it? What if, instead of accepting the narrative that it represents control, we reclaimed its original purpose? What if the eye was never meant to watch over us, but to remind us to watch for ourselves?

Symbols carry power, but that power is shaped by the meaning we assign to them. And sometimes, the key to understanding them is not in what they have become, but in what they were always meant to be.

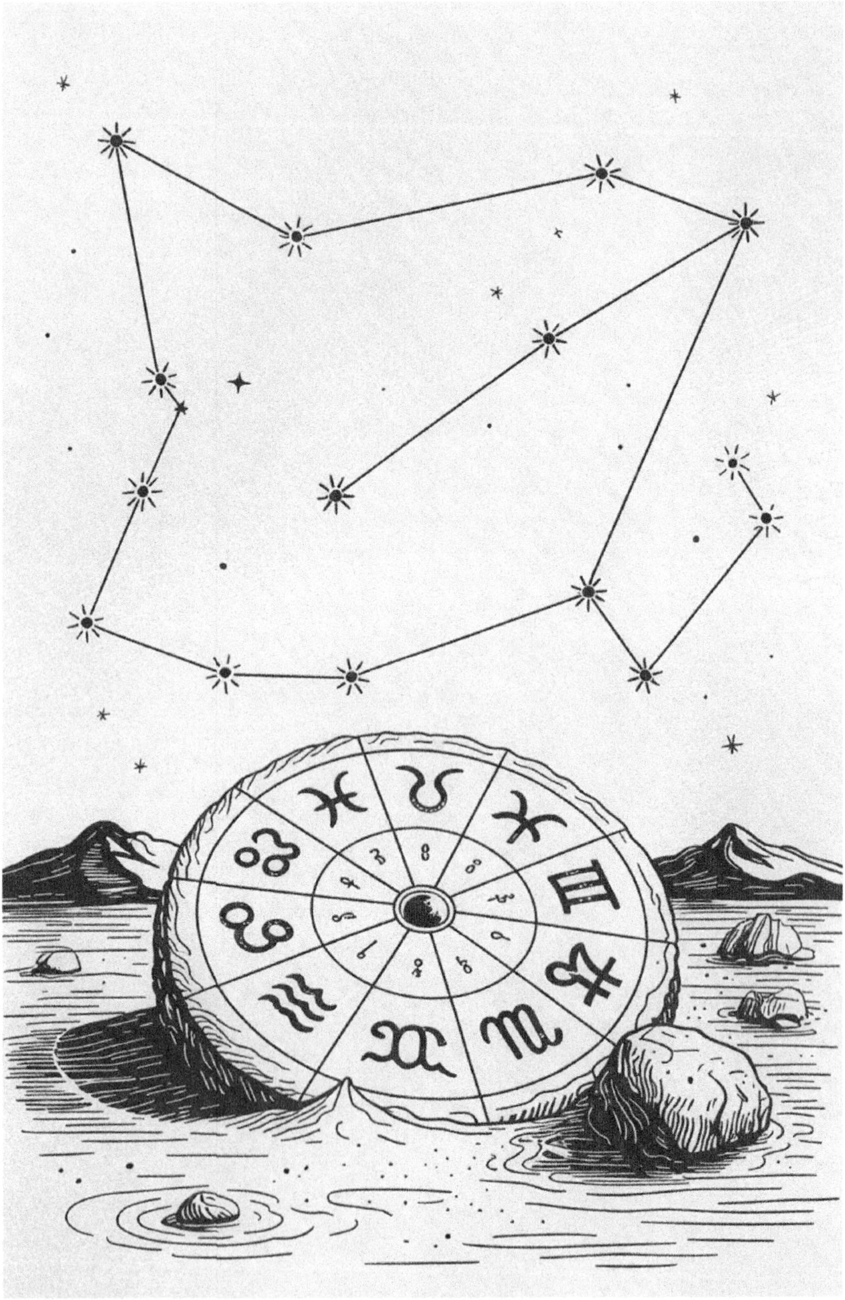

18. *Kundalini energy*, known to yogis for thousands of years and present in Western esoteric traditions, was *ridiculed* and dismissed as "new age fantasy."

Kundalini energy has been spoken of for thousands of years, whispered through the corridors of ancient temples, inscribed in sacred texts, and passed down through esoteric traditions. It was never just an abstract idea, nor merely a metaphor for spiritual awakening. It was described as a real force, a potential that lay dormant within every human being, waiting to be activated. Those who awakened it spoke of profound transformation—visions, altered states of consciousness, an overwhelming sense of unity with the universe.

Yet, in the modern world, this knowledge has been pushed aside. It has been ridiculed, dismissed as superstition, relegated to the realm of mystical exaggeration or new age fantasy. Science has largely ignored it, unable to fit it within the framework of what is considered measurable and empirical. Religious institutions have either misunderstood it or condemned it, wary of its implications for personal spiritual sovereignty. The result is that one of the most powerful forces ever described has been forgotten by many, misrepresented by others, and only truly understood by a few.

Ancient yogic traditions spoke of Kundalini as a coiled serpent lying dormant at the base of the spine. When awakened, it was said to rise through the body's energy centers, known as chakras, igniting a process of inner transformation. This energy was believed to unlock heightened perception, expanded awareness, and a deep connection to something beyond the material world. It was not just a theory but an experience—one that countless seekers across time have described with remarkable similarity.

The texts of India, including the Upanishads and the Tantras, describe Kundalini in precise detail. They speak of its movement, its effects, and the methods to awaken it. Some describe it as fire, others as a flowing current of light. It was said to be the force behind extraordinary states of consciousness, the same energy that enlightened sages and mystics across different traditions. But what makes this phenomenon even more intriguing is that it was not limited to India. Similar concepts appear in Taoist practices, in the Hermetic traditions of the West, even in the mystical branches of Christianity and Sufism. There are references to divine fire, sacred breath, and inner illumination, all pointing to the same fundamental idea—that within the human body lies an untapped energy capable of profound transformation.

If this knowledge was so widespread, why was it dismissed? Why did the modern world reject what the ancients seemed to understand so clearly? Part of the answer lies in the shift towards materialism. As science progressed, the focus turned outward, to what could be seen, measured, and quantified. Experiences that could not be replicated in a laboratory were deemed unreliable. The concept of energy flowing through the body, of consciousness expanding beyond physical perception, was considered too unscientific to be taken seriously. What could not be dissected or observed under a microscope was set aside as mere belief, superstition, or delusion.

Another reason for its suppression may have been far more deliberate. Kundalini was not just about spiritual insight—it was about power. It was said to unlock abilities, enhance intuition, and grant an unshakable awareness of one's place in the universe. Such an awakening made individuals less dependent on external authorities, whether religious or political. It encouraged direct experience over blind faith, inner wisdom over imposed doctrine. A society where individuals had direct access to higher states of awareness was a society that was far more difficult to control.

And so, gradually, the knowledge of Kundalini was distorted. It was either trivialized or demonized, either turned into a caricature of new age mysticism or labeled as dangerous. Stories of spontaneous Kundalini awakenings were dismissed as hallucinations or psychological disturbances. Those who spoke openly of it were often met with skepticism or ridicule. And yet, despite all attempts to suppress or discredit it, the phenomenon never disappeared.

Across the world, there are still those who experience the sudden rising of this energy, often without ever having heard of it before. They report sensations of intense heat, vibrations running up the spine, spontaneous shifts in perception, moments of blissful connection followed by periods of deep transformation. Some struggle with the intensity of the experience, feeling overwhelmed by emotions, memories, or visions they cannot explain. Others describe it as the most profound moment of their lives, an encounter with something so real that it makes ordinary reality seem like a shadow in comparison.

Modern research is slowly beginning to catch up with what the ancients already knew. Neurological studies have shown that deep meditation, breathwork, and other practices associated with Kundalini awakening can lead to changes in brain activity, increased connectivity between different regions, and even shifts in neurotransmitter levels. Some researchers speculate that these experiences may be linked to the release of endogenous chemicals, perhaps even dimethyltryptamine (DMT), often referred to as the spirit molecule. While mainstream science remains cautious, the very fact that such studies are being conducted suggests that the conversation is far from over.

There is also a growing interest in Kundalini from those outside of spiritual traditions. Psychologists have noted that many of the symptoms associated with Kundalini awakening—intense energy surges, altered states of consciousness, deep emotional releases—mirror those found in people undergoing profound psychological transformation. Some have suggested that what ancient texts described as Kundalini may be a natural mechanism for human evolution, a built-in process that, when activated, propels an individual into a higher state of awareness.

If this is true, then what does it mean for the future? Have we, as a civilization, been living with an untapped potential, ignoring a force that could change everything about how we understand ourselves and the universe? Is Kundalini merely an anomaly, an accident of biology, or is it something more—a key to something we have long forgotten?

Perhaps the greatest question of all is not whether Kundalini is real, but why so much effort has been made to convince us that it isn't. If this energy has existed for thousands of years, if it has been described across cultures and traditions, if it has been experienced by thousands of people in the modern world, then why is it still treated as myth? Why is something so transformative so little understood?

Maybe the real secret is not that Kundalini exists, but that we were never meant to awaken it.

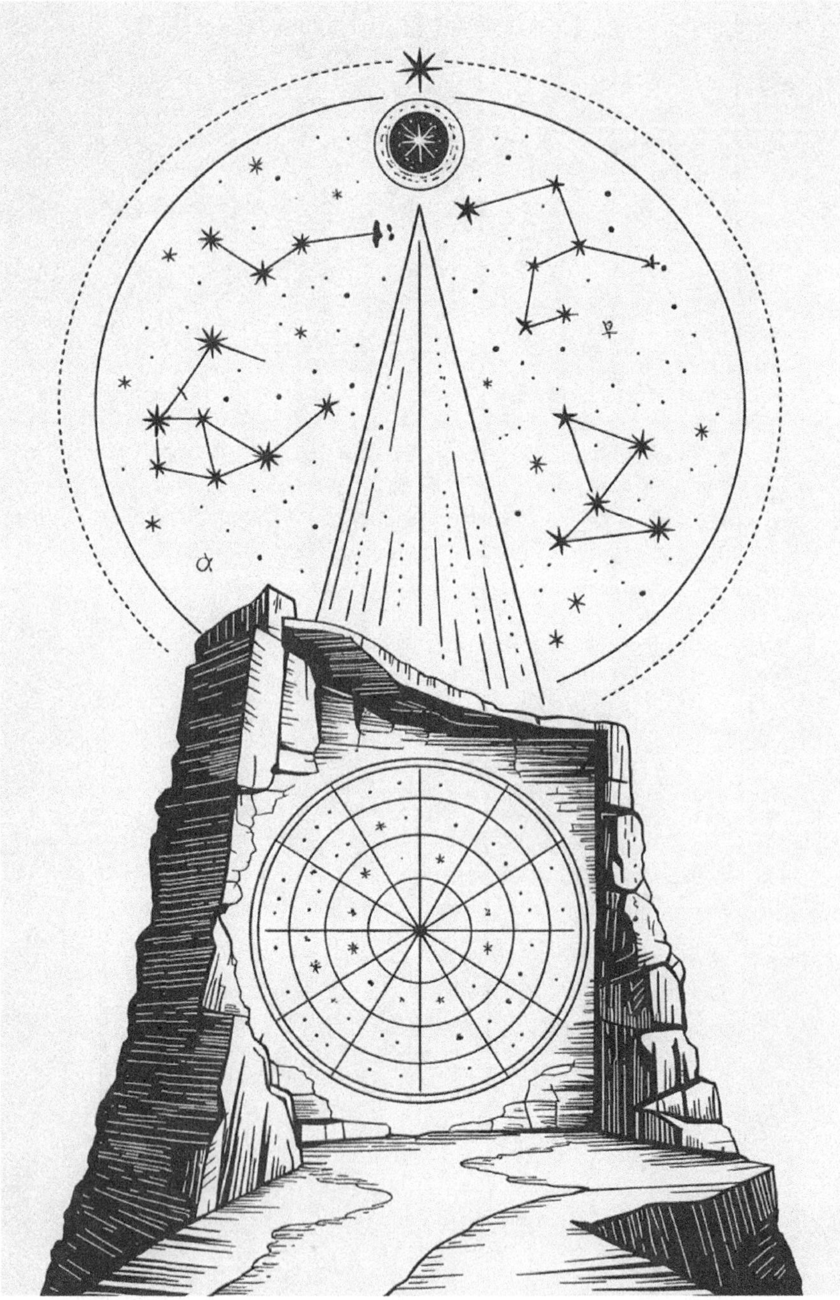

19. *Alchemy*, once a path to the transformation of the soul, was reduced to *witchcraft* and erased from official history.

Alchemy was once regarded as one of the most sacred sciences, a bridge between the material and the divine. It was not merely an attempt to transform lead into gold, as modern interpretations would have people believe. That was only the surface, a veil that concealed a deeper truth. At its core, alchemy was about transformation—the purification of the soul, the mastery of the self, and the unlocking of hidden knowledge embedded within the universe. It was a system of symbols, codes, and metaphysical principles that sought to reveal the secrets of existence, offering those who pursued it a path toward enlightenment.

Yet, over time, this ancient science was reduced to little more than superstition. It was branded as witchcraft, dismissed as primitive chemistry, and eventually erased from official history. The true nature of alchemy, the wisdom contained within its cryptic texts and encoded diagrams, was obscured by layers of misinformation. The question is, why? What was so threatening about alchemy that it needed to be distorted, concealed, or outright destroyed?

The origins of alchemy stretch back thousands of years. Some trace it to ancient Egypt, where it was known as the *Khem* art, a name derived from the dark, fertile soil of the Nile, symbolizing both transformation and creation. The Emerald Tablet, attributed to Hermes Trismegistus, contained the fundamental principles of alchemy, including the famous phrase as above, so below—a concept that suggested a deep connection between the macrocosm of the universe and the microcosm of the human soul. Others point to ancient China, where Taoist alchemists sought the elixir of immortality, blending material experiments with spiritual cultivation. In India, alchemical traditions were tied to the yogic practices of inner transformation, a process not unlike the awakening of Kundalini energy.

Despite their differences, these traditions shared a common understanding. Alchemy was not just about altering substances; it was about *transmuting the self*. The Great Work, as alchemists called it, was a journey of purification, breaking down the lower self to reveal something purer, something luminous. This was symbolized by the philosopher's stone—not a literal object, but a state of being, an inner awakening that granted wisdom, healing, and the ability to perceive reality beyond illusion.

During the Islamic Golden Age, alchemy flourished. Scholars like Jabir ibn Hayyan refined its principles, integrating them with mathematics, astronomy, and medicine. Alchemy was respected, studied, and recognized as both a spiritual and scientific pursuit. Its practitioners were not seen as sorcerers, but as seekers of knowledge, guided by an understanding that the material and the spiritual were deeply intertwined.

Then, something changed.

As Europe entered the medieval period, knowledge became centralized under religious institutions. The Church sought to establish a firm control over what was considered acceptable thought. Alchemy, with its symbols, cryptic texts, and emphasis on self-transformation, was seen as a threat. It encouraged individuals to seek enlightenment outside of established doctrine. It suggested that true power lay not in obedience, but in understanding the hidden forces of nature and the self.

The persecution of alchemists began. Many were forced into secrecy, encoding their wisdom in allegories and symbols to avoid persecution. Some were accused of heresy, others of practicing the dark arts. By the time of the Inquisition, the line between alchemy and witchcraft had been deliberately blurred. What was once a sacred science became associated with superstition, forbidden knowledge, and dangerous experimentation.

This deliberate distortion served a purpose. By reducing alchemy to mere superstition, those in power ensured that its deeper truths would be lost to the masses. If alchemy was seen as nothing more than the foolish pursuit of turning lead into gold, then its real purpose—the transformation of the human soul—would remain hidden. And so, for centuries, alchemy was mocked, dismissed, and excluded from serious intellectual discourse.

Yet, fragments of its wisdom survived. In the Renaissance, figures like Paracelsus and John Dee attempted to revive alchemy, blending it with emerging scientific thought. Isaac Newton, one of the greatest minds of the Enlightenment, secretly studied alchemy, writing extensively on the subject in his private journals. Even as science moved toward materialism, some of the greatest scientists still felt drawn to alchemical principles, sensing that there was something deeper hidden beneath its veiled language.

In modern times, alchemy has been largely forgotten by mainstream culture. It is often portrayed as an outdated pseudoscience, a relic of an era before chemistry and physics provided rational explanations for the workings of the world. But in esoteric circles, the true teachings of alchemy persist. The Great Work is still studied, not as a means to manipulate matter, but as a method for unlocking human potential.

What if alchemy was never meant to be about the external world, but about something far more profound? What if the ancient alchemists encoded their wisdom in symbols and metaphors not to deceive, but to protect? What if they knew that true transformation was not about gold or elixirs, but about unlocking a state of consciousness that would make one truly free?

Perhaps the real question is not whether alchemy worked, but why so much effort was made to convince the world that it didn't.

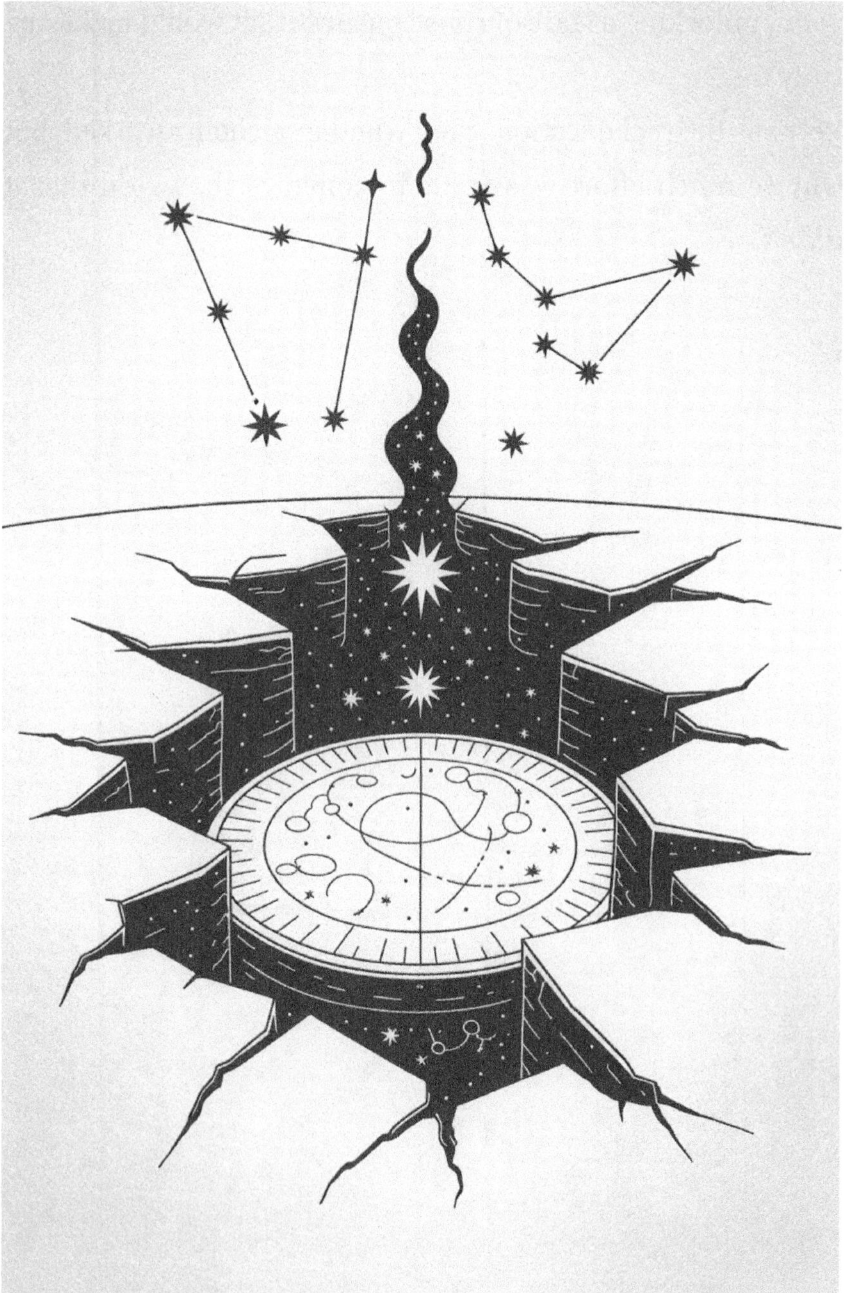

20. The *Vatican Archives* contain thousands of hidden texts—ancient manuscripts, apocryphal gospels, and forbidden knowledge that has never been made public.

The Vatican Archives have long been a source of mystery, speculation, and intrigue. Behind locked doors and beneath heavily guarded halls, thousands of manuscripts remain hidden from public view. These are not ordinary records of history but texts that could change the way humanity understands its past, its spirituality, and its place in the universe.

For centuries, whispers have persisted about what truly lies within these archives. Ancient scrolls, lost gospels, secret correspondences, and esoteric knowledge that has been deliberately concealed. The Church has always justified this secrecy as necessary for preservation, but what if the real reason is something far more complex? What if these texts contain ideas so transformative, so disruptive, that their release would challenge everything we have been told about history, religion, and human potential?

Among the most intriguing of these hidden documents are the apocryphal gospels—writings that were excluded from the official biblical canon. Texts that paint a very different picture of early Christianity, of the teachings of Jesus, and of the spiritual knowledge that was once available to those who sought it. Some of these gospels suggest that Jesus did not preach blind obedience but rather self-realization. That salvation was not granted through external authority, but through direct experience, through inner wisdom, through a deeper understanding of the divine spark within.

These ideas were dangerous. They threatened the structure of institutionalized religion, which required an intermediary between the divine and the people. If individuals could find truth within themselves, if they could access their own spiritual enlightenment without the need for a church hierarchy, the entire foundation of religious authority would be shaken. And so, many of these texts were declared heretical, hidden away, or destroyed.

But what if some survived?

The Vatican Library holds some of the oldest surviving manuscripts in the world. Some believe that among them are documents from the legendary Library of Alexandria, saved before the fires consumed one of the greatest collections of human knowledge. If true, this would mean that records of ancient civilizations, lost philosophies, and forgotten sciences may still exist—records that predate our modern understanding of history.

There are also rumors of esoteric writings, texts that delve into the nature of consciousness, the structure of reality, and the hidden laws of the universe. Some researchers speculate that within these archives could be knowledge about alchemy, energy work, and spiritual transformation—practices that were once considered divine science but have since been dismissed or suppressed.

And then there is the question of extraterrestrial life. Throughout history, the Church has maintained an ambiguous stance on the possibility of civilizations beyond Earth. Yet, some believe that the Vatican possesses records, ancient and modern, that point to knowledge of otherworldly beings. The possibility that ancient texts describe encounters with non-human intelligences, that the Church has been aware of such phenomena for centuries but has chosen not to disclose it, is something that continues to fuel speculation.

Why would such knowledge be hidden? The answer may be simpler than we think. Information is power. The ability to control what people believe about their origins, about their place in the cosmos, about their spiritual potential, is a form of control that surpasses any political or military force. By keeping certain truths concealed, institutions can shape reality itself, guiding humanity along a predefined path.

But secrets have a way of surfacing. Over the centuries, small fragments of these hidden truths have emerged. Discoveries like the Dead Sea Scrolls and the Nag Hammadi texts have given glimpses into early spiritual traditions that differ drastically from the official narratives. They suggest that there was once a much broader and more diverse understanding of the divine, one that was systematically narrowed, edited, and controlled.

The question remains—what else is still hidden? If these archives were truly just a historical record, why the extreme secrecy? Why are so few granted access, even among scholars? What knowledge lies within those walls that the world is not meant to see?

Perhaps the greatest mystery is not just what is contained in the Vatican Archives, but why we have been made to forget that such knowledge ever existed in the first place.

Phase 3 – The Awakening: Reassembling the Fragments of Truth

"The day science begins to study non-physical phenomena, it will make more progress in one decade than in all the previous centuries of its existence."

— Nikola Tesla

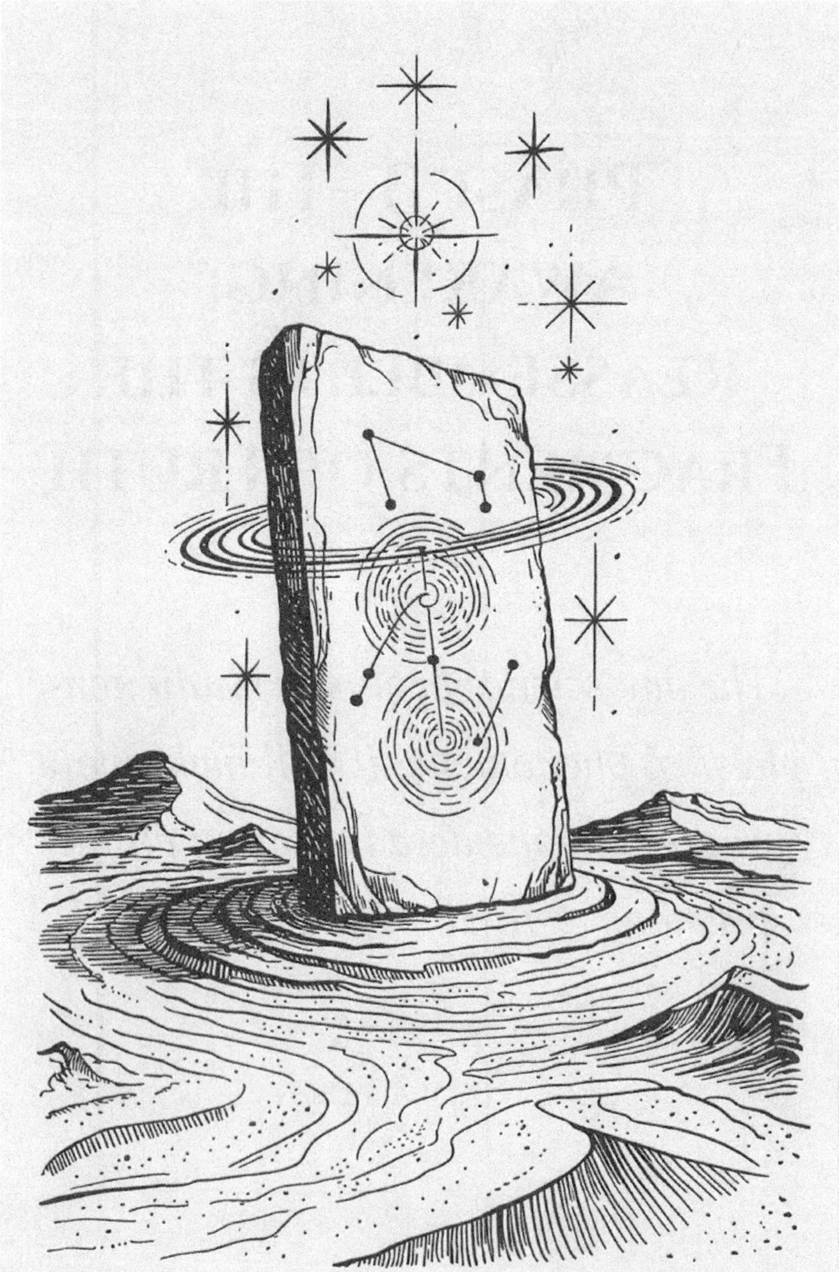

21. *Leonardo da Vinci* wrote in reverse and encoded his works with symbols, as if he knew that certain knowledge had to be hidden from the authorities of his time.

Leonardo da Vinci was more than just an artist, an inventor, or an engineer. He was a man who seemed to exist outside of time, someone whose mind grasped concepts that would take centuries for the rest of the world to understand. His works contain intricate details, hidden meanings, and layers of knowledge that suggest he was operating on a level far beyond that of his contemporaries. But there is something else about him—something more elusive, more enigmatic. He wrote in reverse, he encoded his works with symbols, and he left behind clues that suggest he was aware that certain knowledge had to be concealed.

Why would a man of science and creativity feel the need to disguise his writings? Some believe it was a simple habit, a way to prevent ink smudges as he wrote with his left hand. But others suspect a deeper reason. The time in which Leonardo lived was not kind to those who challenged authority. The Renaissance was an era of discovery, but also of suppression. The Church held immense power, dictating what was acceptable knowledge and what was considered heresy. Any idea that strayed too far from religious doctrine risked not just rejection but persecution.

Leonardo was a man obsessed with knowledge in all its forms. He studied anatomy, dissecting human bodies in secret to understand the mechanics of life. He explored flight, sketching machines that eerily resemble modern aircraft. He examined the properties of water, the movement of the stars, the intricate designs found in nature. His notebooks are filled with observations that seem almost prophetic—drawings of submarines, tanks, and machines that would not be built until centuries later.

If he had discovered something truly groundbreaking, something that could have been seen as a threat to the established order, would he have dared to write it openly? Or would he have hidden it in plain sight, using codes and symbols to conceal his insights from those who might seek to destroy them?

The way Leonardo wrote—mirror writing, flowing from right to left—has long fascinated scholars. Some argue that it was merely a personal quirk, a way to keep his notes private from prying eyes. Others believe it was a deliberate form of encryption, a method of ensuring that only those with the patience and intelligence to decode his words would understand them.

But it was not just his writing that was veiled in secrecy. His paintings, too, contain elements that suggest he was embedding messages, hiding truths beneath layers of oil and pigment. The Mona Lisa, perhaps the most famous painting in the world, has been the subject of endless speculation. Her expression is ambiguous, her gaze almost knowing. Some have claimed that within the details of the painting, Leonardo left hidden symbols, mathematical ratios, even secret messages waiting to be uncovered.

The Last Supper, another of his masterpieces, is filled with anomalies. The positioning of the figures, the hand gestures, the space between them—everything seems carefully arranged as if to communicate something beyond the obvious religious theme. Some theorists suggest that Leonardo was hinting at knowledge that conflicted with the teachings of the Church, that he embedded esoteric wisdom in his art, knowing that it could not be expressed openly.

His fascination with sacred geometry further adds to the mystery. Leonardo was deeply influenced by the golden ratio, a mathematical proportion found throughout nature and often associated with divine perfection. He used this ratio in his works, not just for aesthetic harmony, but perhaps to encode a deeper understanding of the universe.

Then there are his inventions. Many of Leonardo's designs were never built in his lifetime. Some believe this was because the technology of the time was insufficient. Others suspect that he deliberately withheld certain ideas, fearing what might happen if they fell into the wrong hands. A man who could design war machines, who understood the principles of aerodynamics and hydraulics, who had an almost supernatural grasp of anatomy—such a man would have known the dangers of revealing too much too soon.

Could it be that Leonardo da Vinci was not just a visionary, but a man in possession of knowledge that needed to be hidden? Did he write in reverse and use symbols not just out of caution, but because he understood that some truths were not meant for his time?

Perhaps the greatest question of all is what we have yet to uncover. If Leonardo left behind secrets, if his works contain messages still waiting to be deciphered, what might they reveal about the world, about history, about the nature of reality itself? And if such knowledge was deemed too dangerous for the Renaissance, is it still considered too dangerous today?

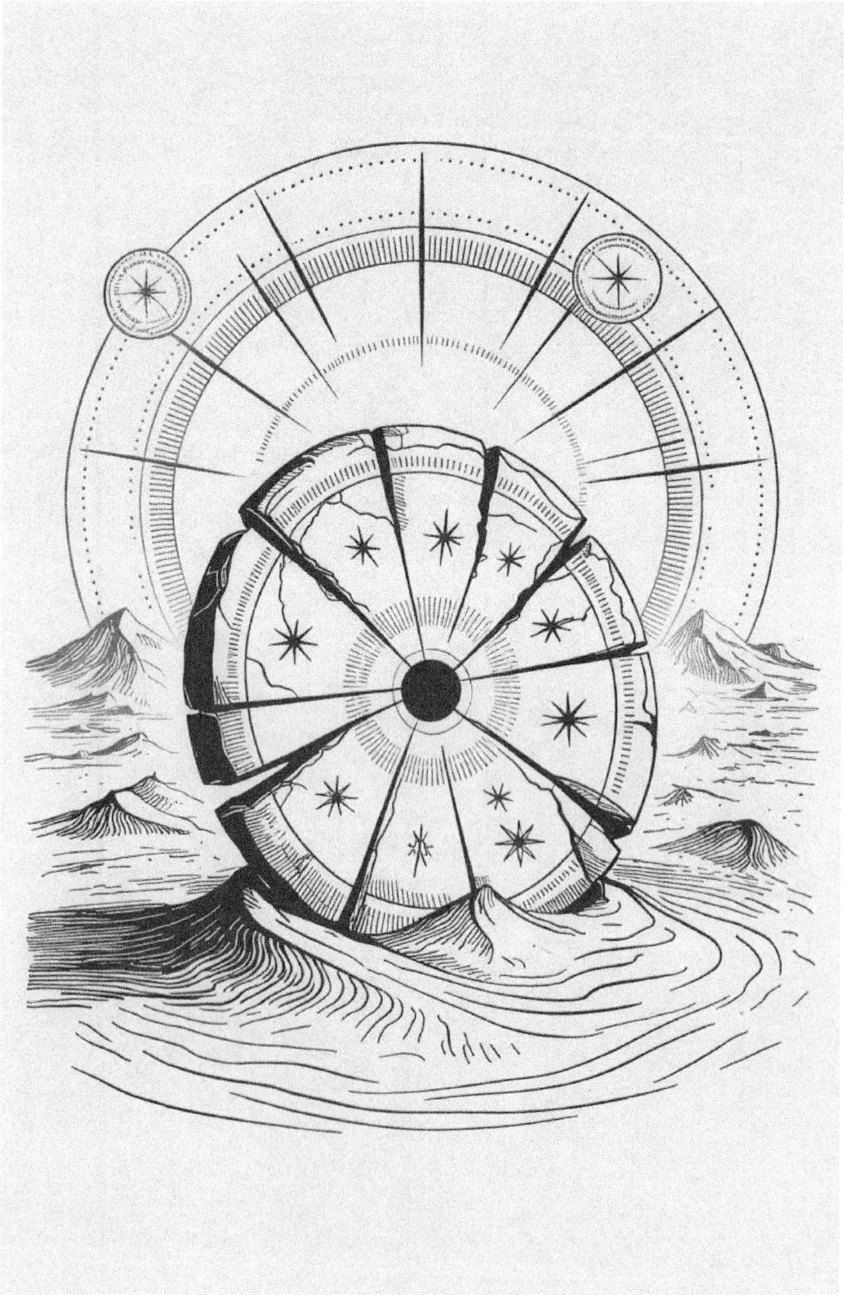

22. Nikola Tesla declared that *the universe operates on energy, frequency, and vibration*—the same fundamental principles at the heart of ancient esoteric traditions.

Nikola Tesla was a man ahead of his time, a visionary who saw beyond the limitations of his era. While the world focused on tangible, mechanical inventions, Tesla was concerned with something far greater—the underlying structure of reality itself. He was not just an inventor but a seeker, a man who believed that the secrets of the universe were encoded in energy, frequency, and vibration.

Throughout his life, Tesla spoke of these principles with unwavering conviction. He claimed that understanding the nature of frequency was the key to unlocking the mysteries of existence. To him, the universe was not a chaotic, random place but a system governed by precise, harmonious laws. He saw patterns in nature, energy in motion, and connections between the visible and the invisible. His insights echoed the wisdom of ancient esoteric traditions—teachings that had been passed down through secret societies, mystery schools, and sacred texts for thousands of years.

The idea that the universe is built on vibration is not new. Hindu philosophy speaks of the primordial sound, the *Om*, as the first vibration that set reality into motion. The Hermetic tradition, traced back to Egypt and Greece, teaches that everything moves, that nothing rests, and that vibration is the fundamental force behind all existence. The teachings of Pythagoras emphasized the relationship between sound, mathematics, and the cosmos, describing the harmony of celestial bodies as a great symphony.

Tesla's discoveries and theories were not mere speculation. He demonstrated that electrical energy could be transmitted wirelessly, that certain frequencies could alter human consciousness, and that power itself could be harnessed from the very fabric of the earth. He envisioned a world where energy was free and limitless, drawn directly from nature rather than being controlled by corporations and governments.

Yet, despite his genius, Tesla's work was systematically buried, his funding cut, his inventions suppressed. Why would a man whose ideas had the potential to revolutionize the world be silenced? Was it simply a matter of business interests, or was there something deeper at play?

Tesla's experiments suggested that energy was not just something to be generated, but something to be *tuned into*. He believed that the Earth itself resonated at a specific frequency, a concept that aligns with the Schumann resonance discovered decades later—the natural electromagnetic frequency of the planet. He understood that sound, electricity, and even thought operated on vibrational principles, and that by learning to manipulate these frequencies, humanity could access new levels of power and awareness.

But such knowledge was dangerous. If the nature of reality could be altered through vibration, if energy could be extracted from the ether itself, what need would there be for fossil fuels, for centralized power grids, for systems of control? Tesla's vision threatened not just industries, but the very foundation of how society was structured. A world where energy was free, where technology was aligned with the deeper forces of nature, was a world that could not be easily governed.

Some of Tesla's most groundbreaking work was lost. His laboratory was mysteriously burned down. After his death, his documents were seized by the government, classified, and hidden away. What was in those papers? What discoveries had he made that were deemed too disruptive to be revealed?

Tesla often spoke of receiving ideas as if they were transmitted to him, not through traditional scientific inquiry, but through direct inspiration. He described moments of intense clarity, visions of complex inventions appearing fully formed in his mind. This phenomenon, too, was not unique to him. Many mystics and spiritual teachers have described knowledge arriving not through linear thought, but through sudden insight, as if tapping into a greater field of consciousness.

If Tesla's understanding of energy, frequency, and vibration was correct, then what does that mean for humanity? Have we been living in an artificially limited reality, disconnected from the deeper forces that govern existence? Could it be that the key to unlocking our potential has been hidden in plain sight, buried beneath layers of scientific dogma and institutional control?

Perhaps Tesla's greatest message was not just about technology, but about perception. If everything is vibration, then our thoughts, emotions, and intentions shape the world around us. If reality is frequency-based, then by shifting our awareness, we can tune into a higher state of being. The implications of this are profound.

What if Tesla was not just an inventor, but a messenger? What if his discoveries were not lost, but waiting to be rediscovered? And if the universe truly operates on energy, frequency, and vibration, then what else might be possible once we learn to harness this forgotten knowledge?

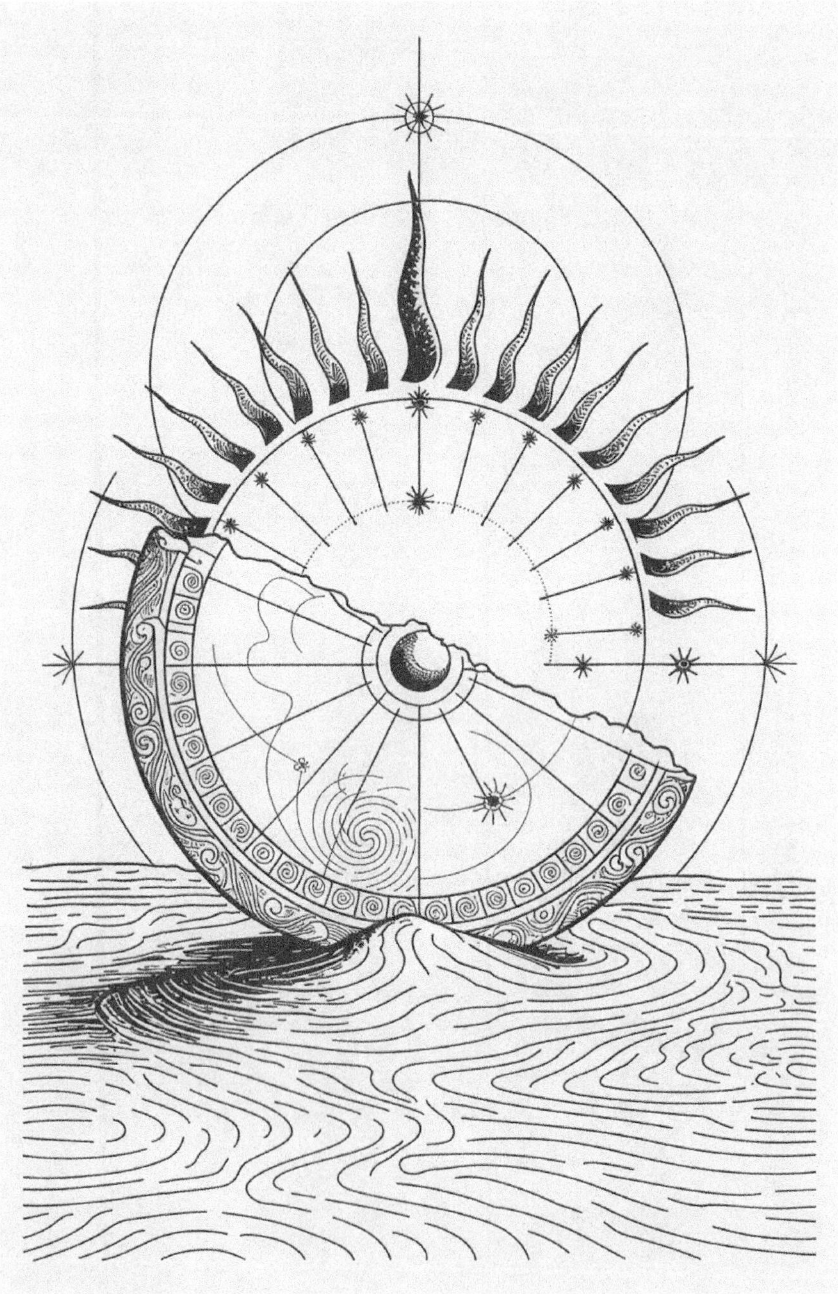

23. The *Fibonacci sequence* and *the Golden Ratio* appear everywhere in nature and sacred architecture, revealing an *underlying order* to the universe.

The universe is not chaos. Beneath the apparent randomness of nature, beneath the vast complexity of galaxies, plants, seashells, and even the structure of the human body, there is a pattern—a rhythm, a sequence that repeats itself again and again, as if reality itself were built upon a hidden code. This code is known as the Fibonacci sequence, a simple yet profound mathematical progression that seems to govern the very fabric of existence. Alongside it, the Golden Ratio, an irrational number approximately equal to 1.618, reveals itself in art, architecture, and the fundamental proportions of life.

The Fibonacci sequence begins with zero and one, and each subsequent number is the sum of the two preceding ones: 0, 1, 1, 2, 3, 5, 8, 13, 21, and so on. At first glance, it appears to be just another mathematical curiosity. But when applied to nature, it becomes something far more mysterious. The spirals of sunflower seeds, the branching of trees, the arrangement of leaves, the shells of nautiluses—all follow

Fibonacci proportions. The galaxies swirling in space mirror the same patterns, as if an invisible hand has used this sequence to shape the cosmos.

But why? Why would nature, in all its diversity, follow such a specific numerical pattern? What underlying principle drives this design? Ancient civilizations seemed to have understood that there was something special about these numbers, something sacred. The Egyptians incorporated the Golden Ratio into the construction of the Great Pyramid of Giza. The Greeks used it in the Parthenon. The architects of Gothic cathedrals embedded it into their designs, believing that it brought their structures into harmony with divine proportions.

Leonardo da Vinci was fascinated by the Golden Ratio, which he called the divine proportion. He saw it in the proportions of the human body, in the design of faces, in the architecture of nature itself. His famous drawing, the Vitruvian Man, depicts a human figure perfectly aligned with geometric ratios that reflect this same principle. Was he merely observing a mathematical curiosity, or had he uncovered a fundamental truth about reality?

The deeper one looks, the more the presence of these numbers becomes undeniable. The Fibonacci sequence is found in DNA, the genetic code that forms the foundation of all life. It appears in the proportions of the human face, the length of bones, the structure of hurricanes. Even financial markets seem to move in patterns that align with Fibonacci retracement levels, as if human behavior itself is influenced by these ancient principles.

But perhaps the most intriguing question is not just where these patterns appear, but why they exist at all. Are they a coincidence, a mere mathematical accident? Or do they reveal something deeper, something about the very nature of existence? If the same sequence governs the growth of a pinecone, the spirals of a galaxy, and the architecture of ancient temples, does this suggest that everything is connected by a common structure, a hidden order that permeates reality?

Some have speculated that these ratios are not just an observation of nature's design, but the fingerprint of a greater intelligence. Could it be that the Fibonacci sequence and the Golden Ratio are not human discoveries at all, but glimpses into the underlying code of the universe? If so, what does this imply about our place within it?

Mystics and philosophers have long suggested that numbers are more than mere tools for measurement. Pythagoras, the ancient Greek mathematician and philosopher, believed that numbers were the foundation of all reality. To him, the universe was not built from matter but from vibrations, ratios, and harmonics. The Golden Ratio, in his view, was not just a proportion but a key to understanding the harmony of the cosmos.

In modern times, science has confirmed what the ancients seemed to intuitively understand. Studies in fractal geometry, chaos theory, and quantum mechanics suggest that nature is built upon recursive patterns, that what appears to be disorder is, in fact, an intricate design. The Fibonacci sequence and the Golden Ratio are not isolated curiosities; they are woven into the very structure of existence, from the smallest particles to the vastness of the universe.

Yet, despite their presence everywhere, these patterns remain largely unexplored in mainstream discourse. Schools teach the Fibonacci sequence as a mathematical exercise, rarely touching upon its deeper implications. Architects use the Golden Ratio for aesthetic appeal, often without questioning why it is so pleasing to the human eye. Science acknowledges its existence but hesitates to ask the larger question: why is reality structured this way?

Perhaps the answer lies not in numbers alone, but in perception. What if these patterns are not just mathematical rules, but a clue—an invitation to see the world differently? If the universe is built upon a precise, recurring structure, what does that say about free will, about destiny, about the nature of consciousness itself? Are we participants in this pattern, or are we its creators?

If everything follows a mathematical blueprint, then what else might be governed by the same principles? Do thoughts, emotions, and events move in Fibonacci-like cycles? Is there a hidden rhythm to time, to history, to the unfolding of human experience? And if we could recognize these patterns, could we learn to navigate them, to anticipate the flow of reality itself?

Perhaps the Fibonacci sequence and the Golden Ratio are more than just numbers. Perhaps they are a key, a glimpse into a greater truth—one that has always been there, waiting for those who are ready to see.

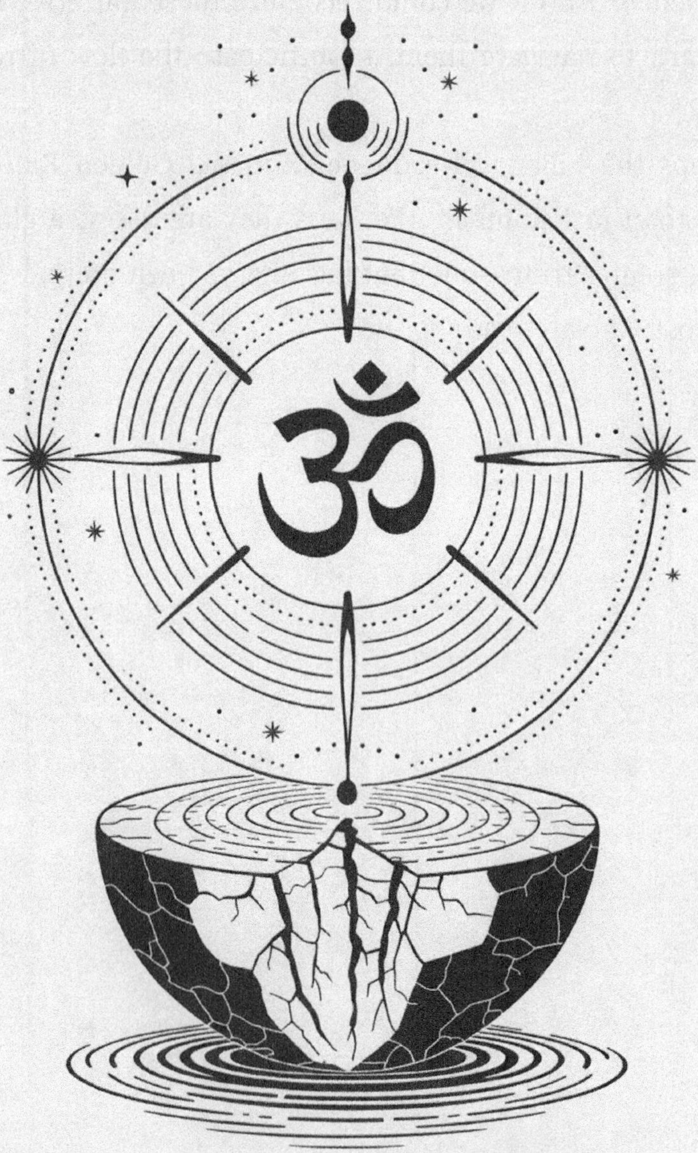

24. The sacred sound *OM*, chanted in Eastern traditions, resonates at frequencies that *harmonize the body and mind,* reflecting the primordial vibration of creation.

The sound *Om* has been chanted for thousands of years, its deep, resonant vibration echoing through temples, meditation halls, and sacred spaces. It is considered the primordial sound, the vibration from which all existence emerges, the frequency that connects everything in the universe. But beyond its spiritual significance, *Om* carries something deeper—an energy that seems to influence the body, the mind, and even the fabric of reality itself.

Ancient Indian traditions describe *Om* as the *pranava*, the eternal sound, the first breath of creation. The Vedas, some of the oldest known scriptures, state that the universe was not created by a physical force but by vibration, by a resonance that brought form out of formlessness. Modern science, in its own way, has arrived at a similar conclusion. Quantum physics suggests that everything is energy, that at the most fundamental level, reality is not solid matter but waves, frequencies, vibrations in motion.

If the universe is built on vibration, then sound becomes more than just an auditory experience. It becomes a force, a way of shaping reality itself. This is something the ancients understood intuitively. The chanting of *Om* was not simply a ritual; it was a means of aligning with the fundamental frequency of existence. It was a way to resonate with the cosmos, to tune the human system to the deeper rhythms that govern all things.

When chanted correctly, *Om* creates a vibration that flows through the body, resonating in the chest, the throat, and the head. Studies in modern acoustics have shown that this sound produces a measurable effect, calming the nervous system, reducing stress, and creating a state of deep focus and relaxation. Brainwave studies have demonstrated that chanting *Om* shifts the brain into an alpha state, the same frequency associated with meditation, intuition, and heightened awareness.

But what if this effect is more than just biological? What if *Om* does not simply calm the mind but actually connects the individual to something greater? Ancient texts describe *Om* as the sound of the universe itself, the vibration that underlies all creation. In some traditions, it is said that by chanting *Om*, one aligns with the divine, with the unseen structure of reality. There is evidence to suggest that sound has the power to shape matter. The science of cymatics, which studies how sound frequencies affect physical structures, has revealed astonishing patterns. When certain frequencies are played through a medium like sand or water, they form intricate geometric shapes, some of which resemble sacred symbols found in spiritual traditions across the world. Could it be that the sound of *Om* creates similar patterns, not just externally but within the body, within the energy field, within consciousness itself?

The ancient sages believed that everything has a frequency, that health, thought, and even emotions are governed by vibration. Disease, in this view, was seen as a distortion of one's natural frequency, and healing involved restoring harmony. This idea is mirrored in modern sound therapy, where specific tones are used to balance the mind and body.

If sound has the ability to heal, if it can create order out of chaos, then what role does *Om* play in this process? Could it be that chanting *Om* is a way to recalibrate the system, to restore lost harmony? Many who practice this chant report feelings of deep peace, an altered sense of time, even moments of profound insight. Some describe it as a gateway, a way to tap into something beyond ordinary perception.

Across cultures, variations of the *Om* sound appear in spiritual traditions. The *Aum* of Hinduism, the *Amen* of Christianity, the *Amin* of Islam—all carry a similar resonance, as if different civilizations, separated by geography and time, arrived at the same understanding through different means.

Could it be that these sacred sounds are all reflections of the same fundamental vibration?

If the universe is sound, if reality itself is built on frequency, then perhaps *Om* is more than just a word. Perhaps it is a key, a tool, a reminder of something humanity once knew but has since forgotten.

What if the power of *Om* is not in the sound itself, but in the recognition of what it represents? What if by chanting it, by feeling its vibration within, one is not just calming the mind but reconnecting with the source of all things? And if that is true, then how much more of reality might be shaped by sound, by intention, by vibration?

Perhaps *Om* is not simply a chant. Perhaps it is an invitation—to listen, to feel, and to remember.

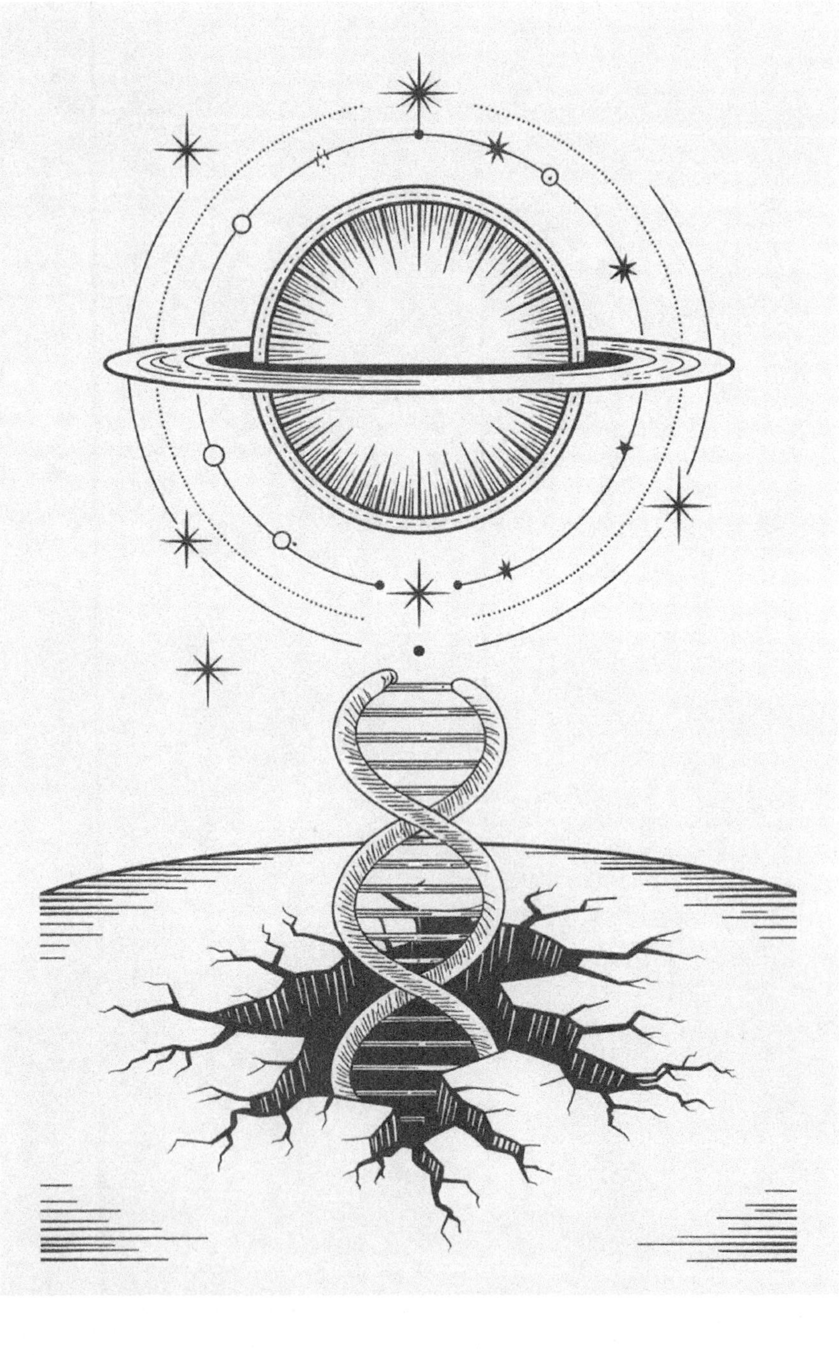

25. *Human DNA responds to sound, emotions, and intention* — exactly as ancient spiritual teachings described the *creative power of the word.*

For centuries, spiritual traditions have spoken of the power of words, of sound, of intention. They have taught that the universe itself was spoken into existence, that reality responds to vibration, that the very fabric of human life is shaped by the frequencies we emit. Science, for a long time, dismissed these ideas as metaphors, as poetic descriptions rather than literal truths. But as research advances, something remarkable is emerging—human DNA, the very blueprint of life, appears to respond to sound, emotions, and intention in ways that align with ancient wisdom.

At the heart of many religious traditions is the belief that words hold power. In the Gospel of John, it is written that in the beginning was the Word, and the Word was with God, and the Word was God. In Hinduism, the sacred sound Om is said to be the vibration from which all creation emerged. The ancient Egyptians believed that words, spoken with the right intention, could alter reality itself. These ideas, once considered mystical, are now finding parallels in modern scientific discoveries.

DNA is often thought of as a static, unchangeable code, a biological script that determines who we are. But this view is being challenged. Studies in epigenetics have shown that DNA is not fixed—it responds to the environment, to emotions, to consciousness itself. The very structure of our genetic material can shift, activate, or silence certain genes based on external influences. And among those influences, sound and intention appear to play a crucial role.

In the 1990s, Russian researchers made a discovery that shocked the scientific world. They found that the DNA molecule, far from being an isolated biological structure, behaves like an antenna, capable of receiving and transmitting information. Linguistic analysis of DNA sequences revealed that the genetic code follows patterns similar to human language. This suggested something extraordinary—our DNA is structured not just like a chemical blueprint, but like a form of communication, a biological script that can be rewritten.

More astonishingly, experiments indicated that specific frequencies of sound could directly affect DNA, altering its function. Low-frequency vibrations could repair damaged strands, while certain spoken words, when infused with intention, appeared to trigger measurable changes. This aligns with what many ancient traditions have always taught—that sound is not just heard, but felt, absorbed, and integrated into the body.

Emotions, too, have been shown to influence genetic expression. Studies have demonstrated that states of gratitude, love, and compassion enhance cellular function, while prolonged stress, fear, and negativity cause damage at the molecular level. The work of researchers like Dr. Masaru Emoto further supports this idea. His experiments on water molecules revealed that words and emotions could alter the crystalline structure of water, forming beautiful symmetrical patterns when exposed to positive words and distorted, chaotic shapes when exposed to negative ones. Given that the human body is composed largely of water, the implications are profound.

If sound, thought, and intention can influence the molecules of water, what effect might they have on the human body as a whole? And if DNA itself responds to these influences, could it be that our very essence, our genetic identity, is more fluid, more responsive, than we have been led to believe?

Ancient teachings have long emphasized the power of the spoken word. Mantras, prayers, affirmations—these were not just rituals, but technologies of consciousness, designed to realign the self with higher frequencies. Shamans and healers across cultures have used chants and tonal vibrations to restore health, recognizing that illness often begins as an energetic imbalance. Even in modern medicine, sound frequencies are being explored for their potential to heal, from ultrasound therapy to the emerging field of bioacoustics.

This raises deeper questions about the nature of reality itself. If DNA responds to sound and intention, then consciousness is not merely an observer of life—it is a participant, a creator. The human voice, when used with intention, becomes a tool of transformation. Words cease to be passive and become active forces, capable of shaping the world around us.

If everything is vibration, then our thoughts, emotions, and speech are constantly sending signals, constantly interacting with the unseen structure of existence. Could it be that the ability to reshape our reality has always been within us, encoded in our very being?

Perhaps this is why so many ancient traditions placed such importance on silence, on choosing words carefully, on the understanding that what we speak shapes what we experience. Perhaps this is why curses and blessings were taken so seriously, why initiates were trained in the discipline of speech, why sacred chants were preserved with such precision.

What we call science and what we call spirituality may not be so different after all. One explores the external world, the other the internal. But at their core, both seek the same truth—that we are not separate from the universe, but woven into its design. And if DNA, the very foundation of human life, responds to sound and intention, then the power to transform is not something we must seek outside ourselves. It is already within us, waiting to be awakened.

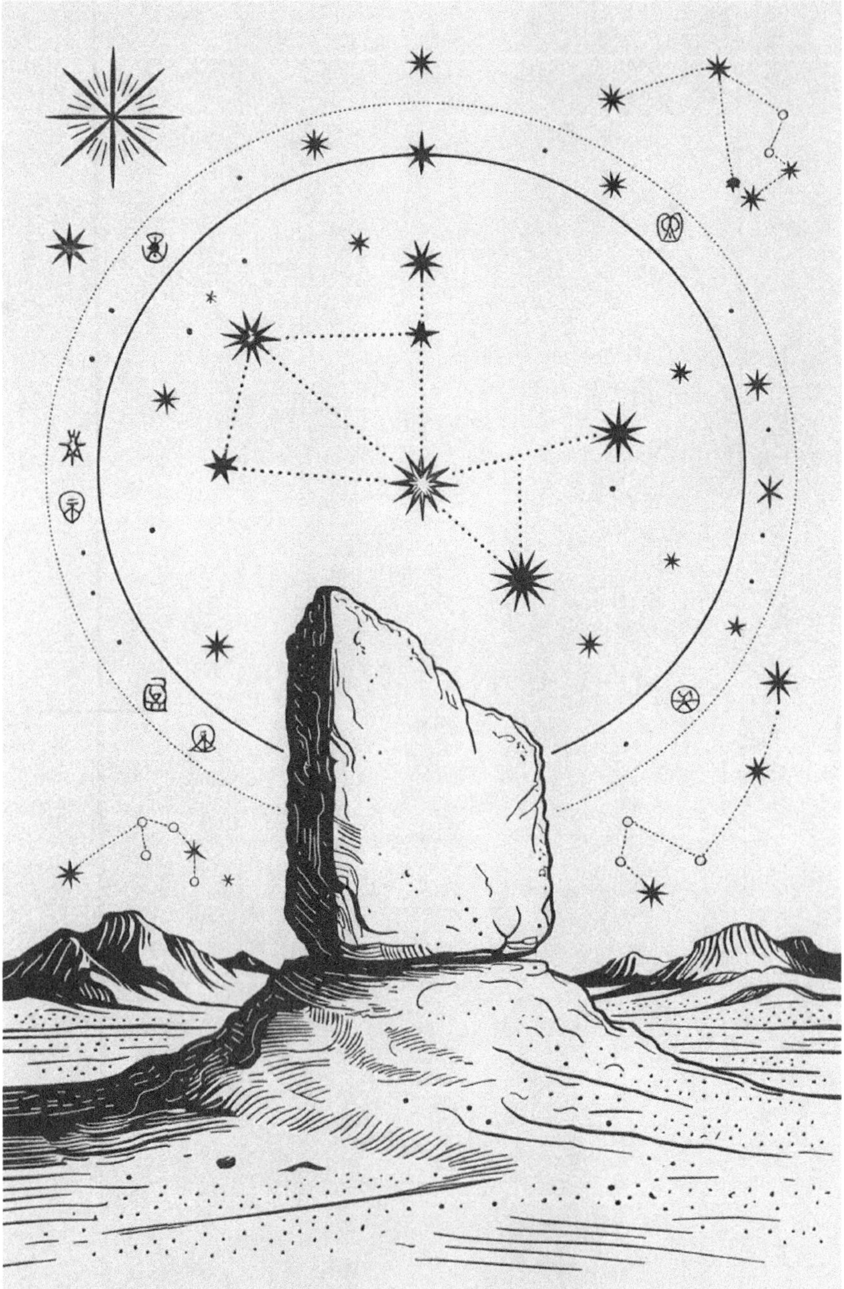

26. The *Dogon people of Mali* knew of *Sirius B*—a star invisible without telescopes—long before modern astronomy confirmed its existence. Where did this knowledge come from?

The Dogon people of Mali hold one of the most perplexing and controversial pieces of ancient knowledge ever recorded. A seemingly isolated tribe, living in the rugged cliffs and desert landscapes of West Africa, they possess an astronomical understanding that should have been impossible for a pre-modern society. At the heart of this mystery is their knowledge of Sirius B, a star invisible to the naked eye, hidden within the brightness of its larger companion, Sirius A. Modern astronomers only confirmed its existence in the 19th century, yet the Dogon had already encoded its presence into their sacred traditions for generations.

How could a people without telescopes, without written records of scientific discovery, know about a celestial body that required advanced optics and physics to detect? The implications of this question are profound, challenging the conventional view of how knowledge is acquired, transmitted, and preserved.

For the Dogon, the knowledge of Sirius B is not a recent discovery but part of an ancient tradition passed down through oral teachings and sacred rituals. Their myths speak of a time when their ancestors were visited by beings known as the Nommo—described as amphibious, fish-like entities that came from the sky. These beings, according to Dogon lore, were responsible for imparting wisdom, including information about the stars. The Dogon describe Sirius B as a companion to Sirius A, orbiting it in an elliptical path over a period of approximately 50 years—a fact that modern astronomy only confirmed with advanced measurements and mathematical modeling.

The Dogon's knowledge extends beyond just recognizing Sirius B. They speak of it as an extremely dense, heavy star, something that was verified only in the 20th century when astronomers classified it as a white dwarf, one of the densest forms of matter known. Their traditions also include references to a third star in the Sirius system, which, interestingly, remains unconfirmed by modern science but has been theorized by some researchers.

How did they come to possess this information? Mainstream historians often argue that the Dogon could have gained their knowledge through contact with European travelers or missionaries. Yet, this explanation fails to account for the depth of their astronomical understanding, which includes complex descriptions of planetary motion, the phases of

Venus, and even the spiral structure of the Milky Way—concepts that were not part of mainstream Western astronomy until relatively recently.

Another theory suggests that this knowledge is a remnant of an ancient, now-lost civilization. Some researchers propose that early African cultures may have been part of a wider network of advanced knowledge, one that predated written history and was passed down through oral tradition. If so, the Dogon may not be an anomaly but a surviving link to an earlier age of scientific awareness.

Then there is the possibility, more controversial yet deeply fascinating, that their knowledge comes from precisely where they claim it did—from an external intelligence, from beings who arrived long ago and shared their wisdom. Across multiple cultures, myths describe gods, sky beings, or celestial visitors who came down to teach humanity. From the Sumerian Anunnaki to the feathered serpents of Mesoamerica, the theme of knowledge being handed down from the stars is a recurring one.

If the Dogon's story is true—if their ancestors did indeed receive teachings from an advanced civilization, whether terrestrial or extraterrestrial—then the implications are staggering. It would suggest that our understanding of history is incomplete, that human civilization may have been shaped by influences we have yet to fully comprehend.

Some skeptics argue that the Dogon's knowledge of Sirius B has been exaggerated or misinterpreted. They claim that anthropologists who studied the Dogon may have inadvertently influenced their stories, inserting modern astronomical concepts into their mythology. Yet, this perspective does not account for the depth of Dogon cosmology, which includes intricate knowledge of celestial cycles, orbital mechanics, and galactic structures. Their traditions are not a collection of vague star myths but a detailed and precise system of astronomical understanding.

In recent years, interest in the Dogon's knowledge has expanded beyond academia. The idea that ancient cultures possessed advanced scientific wisdom—either through forgotten civilizations or through external contact—has gained traction. Some researchers point to the alignments of megalithic structures, the precision of ancient calendars, and the sudden emergence of high-level mathematical and engineering skills in early human history as indications that we may be missing a key chapter in our past.

The Dogon mystery is not just about astronomy. It is about the nature of knowledge itself. If a remote African tribe preserved information about an invisible star long before it was known to modern science, what else might be hidden in ancient traditions? What other pieces of knowledge, dismissed as myth, could one day be validated?

Perhaps the real lesson of the Dogon is not just that they knew of Sirius B, but that history is far more complex than we assume. Knowledge, it seems, does not always follow the linear progression we have been taught. Sometimes, it survives in the most unexpected places, waiting for the world to catch up.

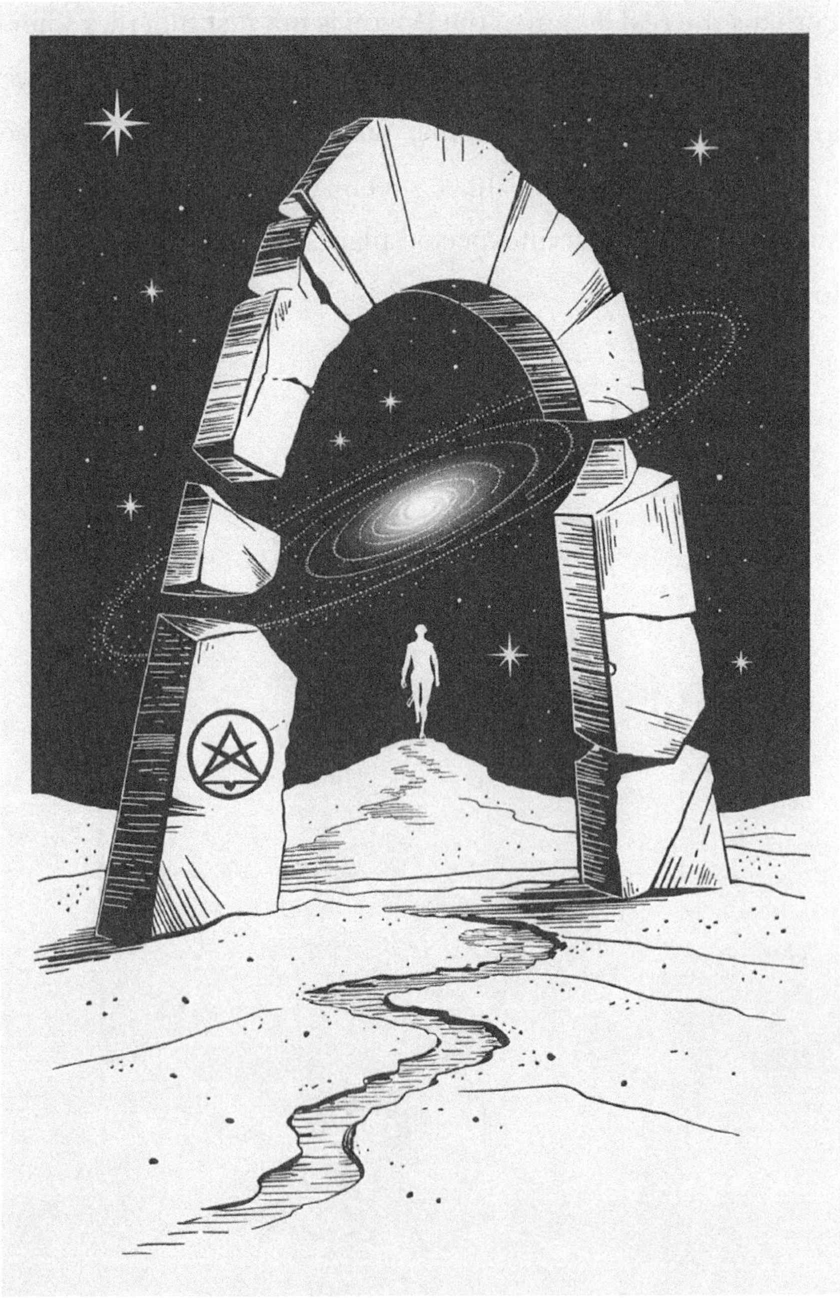

27. *Gnosticism* teaches that *the material world is an illusion,* a prison created by a *Demiurge,* and that true divinity resides *within* us, not in external gods.

Gnosticism is not merely a religious philosophy; it is a radical challenge to the nature of reality itself. It does not ask followers to believe in an external god, nor does it promise salvation through obedience to religious institutions. Instead, it teaches something far more unsettling—that the world as we perceive it is an illusion, a prison designed to keep humanity trapped in ignorance. The true divine spark, the essence of what we are, is not found in distant heavens, nor is it bestowed by any godly ruler. It has always been within us, waiting to be remembered.

At its core, Gnosticism presents a vision of existence that is both deeply mystical and profoundly subversive. Unlike mainstream religious traditions, which portray creation as an act of divine benevolence, Gnostic teachings suggest that the material world was not created by a true god, but by a Demiurge—a false deity, an imposter who constructed reality as a place of limitation, suffering, and deception. This Demiurge, often associated with the Old Testament god, is not a loving creator but a ruler who keeps souls bound in a cycle of illusion. The physical universe, according to Gnostics, is a trap. And like any good trap, it was built to be convincing.

If the world is a prison, then what are we? The Gnostics taught that within every human being lies a fragment of something beyond this false reality—a divine spark, a remnant of a greater existence that predates material creation. This spark is the key to escaping the illusion, but most people live their entire lives unaware of its presence. The structures of society, the distractions of everyday existence, the endless pursuit of power, wealth, and status—these are not coincidences. They are mechanisms of control, designed to keep humanity from looking inward, from remembering what has been forgotten.

The path to liberation, according to Gnosticism, is not through worship, obedience, or external rituals. It is through *gnosis*— a direct, experiential knowledge of reality as it truly is. This knowledge is not intellectual, nor can it be taught in the conventional sense. It must be realized, awakened within. Those who attain gnosis do not merely believe in a higher truth; they *see* it. And once seen, the illusion of the material world can never again hold them in its grasp.

Ancient Gnostic texts, such as those found in the Nag Hammadi library, reveal a strikingly different interpretation of religious figures and events. In the Gnostic Gospel of Thomas, Jesus does not present himself as a savior in the traditional sense. Instead, he acts as a guide, reminding his followers that the kingdom of God is *not* a distant paradise, but something already present—within them. The message is clear: the divine is not something to be sought outside oneself, but something to be uncovered within. This teaching, however, was seen as dangerous by early religious authorities. If individuals could connect directly to the divine, what need was there for priests, for churches, for intermediaries who claimed to hold the keys to salvation?

It is no coincidence that Gnostic teachings were suppressed, labeled as heresy, and nearly wiped from history. They posed a direct threat to the rising power of organized religion. The idea that the material world was a deception, that the god worshipped by mainstream traditions was a false ruler, that true enlightenment required looking inward rather than upward—these concepts could not be allowed to spread. And so, Gnostic texts were banned, their followers persecuted, their wisdom buried beneath centuries of dogma.

Yet, fragments of Gnosticism survived, hidden in esoteric traditions, encoded in myths, and carried forward by those who refused to accept the illusion. The Cathars of medieval France embraced a Gnostic worldview, seeing the material world as corrupt and rejecting the authority of the Church. The Kabbalists of Jewish mysticism explored similar themes, describing a fragmented reality in which divine sparks must be reunited with their source. Even in modern times, echoes of Gnosticism can be found in philosophy, literature, and psychology. The idea that reality is not as it seems, that we are trapped in a construct designed to keep us from our true nature, continues to resurface in different forms.

Science, too, has begun to touch upon ideas that align with ancient Gnostic thought. The study of quantum mechanics suggests that reality is far less solid, far less objective than once believed. The observer effect, the nature of consciousness, the illusion of time—these mysteries hint at a universe that is not as fixed as it appears. Could it be that the Gnostics intuited something that science is only now beginning to explore? If the world is an illusion, then what exists beyond it? If our consciousness is trapped within this material construct, then where did it originate?

Perhaps the most challenging aspect of Gnosticism is its demand for awakening. It does not offer easy answers, nor does it provide comfort in the way traditional religions do. To accept Gnostic teachings is to accept responsibility for one's own liberation. There is no external savior, no divine force that will come to rescue us from the illusion. The only way out is through knowledge—through the difficult, often painful process of seeing beyond the veil and reclaiming the divine spark that has been hidden.

But what if this knowledge is not just an ancient philosophy? What if it is a map—one that was left behind for those willing to see? What if the world is not what it seems, and the only way to escape is to remember what we were before the illusion took hold? If true divinity is within, then what else have we forgotten? And if the Gnostics were right, then who—or what—really rules the world we think we know?

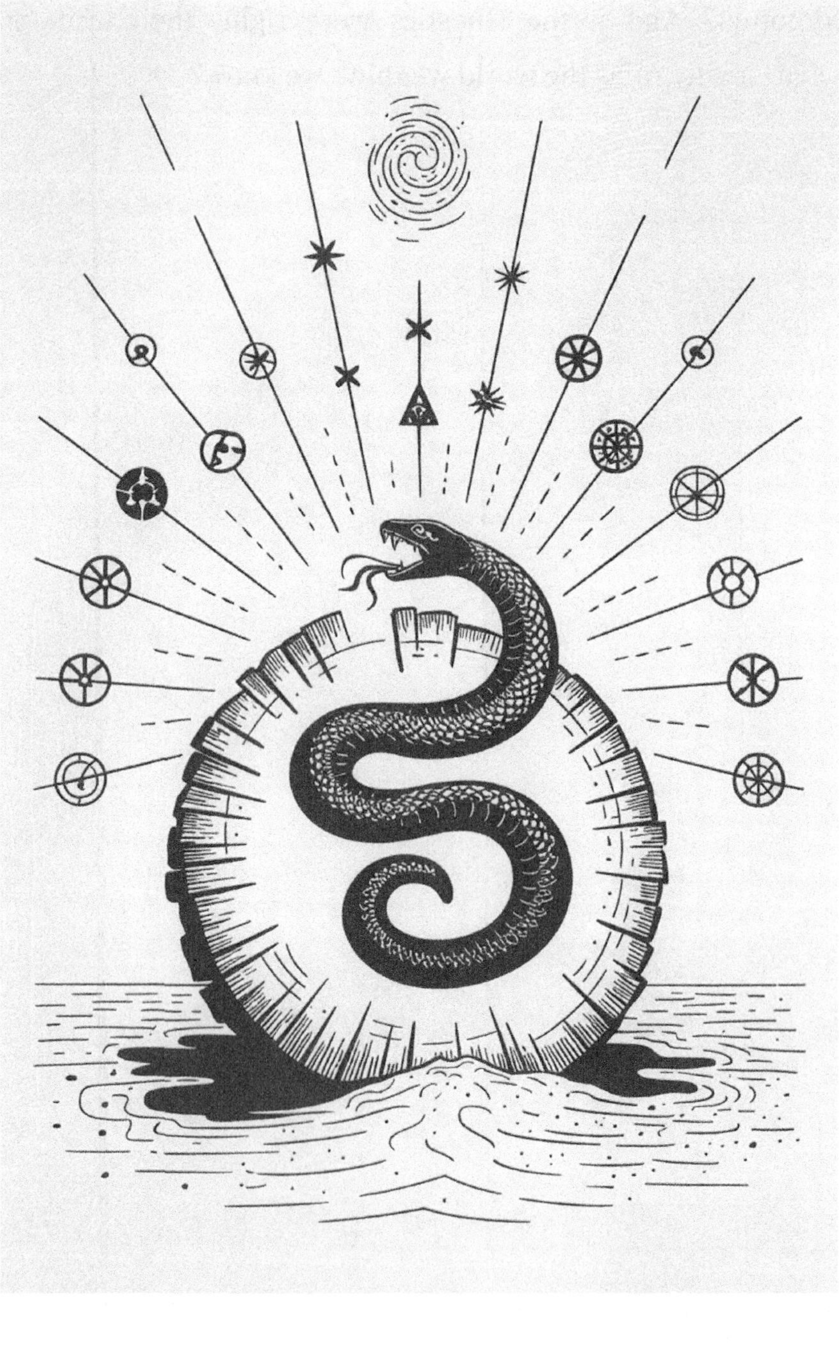

28. The *Ouroboros*, the serpent eating its own tail, appears in ancient civilizations worldwide—evidence of a *universal hidden truth* that transcends borders and eras.

The image of a serpent devouring its own tail has endured across cultures, epochs, and civilizations. Known as the Ouroboros, this enigmatic symbol appears in Egyptian papyri, Greek alchemical texts, Norse mythology, Hindu traditions, and even in esoteric Renaissance thought. How could such a precise, deeply symbolic image emerge in civilizations separated by vast distances and time? What secret knowledge did it carry that made it so universally significant?

At first glance, the Ouroboros appears simple—just a snake or dragon forming a perfect circle, consuming itself in an endless loop. But its meaning is anything but simple. It is a paradox, a contradiction that reveals a hidden truth. It represents the cycle of life and death, creation and destruction, beginning and end as one. The serpent consumes itself, yet it is never truly gone. It renews itself in an eternal cycle, symbolizing regeneration, alchemy, and the infinite nature of existence.

The earliest known depiction of the Ouroboros comes from ancient Egypt, appearing in the tomb of Pharaoh Tutankhamun. In Egyptian belief, the Ouroboros was associated with *Atum*, the primordial deity who brought the universe into being. It represented the cyclical nature of time, the endless renewal of the cosmos. It also appeared in funerary texts, symbolizing the eternal journey of the soul beyond death. The Egyptians understood time not as a straight line, but as a repeating cycle—an idea that would persist in many ancient cultures.

In Greece, the Ouroboros took on an alchemical and philosophical meaning. The philosopher Heraclitus wrote of a world in constant transformation, a universe shaped by fire, destruction, and rebirth. The Ouroboros embodied this principle, illustrating the concept that everything must consume itself to be reborn anew. Greek alchemists adopted the symbol as a representation of the ultimate unity of all things—the idea that opposites, rather than being separate, are inextricably linked. Light and dark, life and death, creation and dissolution are not opposing forces but different aspects of the same eternal process.

The Norse myths also contain echoes of the Ouroboros. The great serpent *Jörmungandr*, a child of Loki, encircles the world, biting its own tail. It is said that when it finally releases its grip, Ragnarok—the end of the world—will begin. Here, too, the image suggests cycles: the destruction of one world leads to the birth of another. Nothing is ever truly lost; it is merely transformed.

In Hinduism, the concept of endless cycles is embedded in the very fabric of reality. The universe moves through repeated creations and destructions, known as *kalpas*, immense cosmic cycles that mirror the endless turning of the Ouroboros. In some depictions of the god Vishnu, a serpent coils around him, suggesting infinity and the cosmic order that governs existence.

But perhaps the most intriguing aspect of the Ouroboros is not just that it appears in different civilizations, but that it seems to encode a deeper understanding of reality—one that modern science is only beginning to grasp. The idea that everything is interconnected, that destruction is not an end but a transformation, aligns closely with quantum physics, thermodynamics, and even the structure of DNA.

Some scholars have speculated that the Ouroboros represents the structure of the universe itself. The physicist Nassim Haramein has suggested that the fundamental nature of reality may be toroidal—a self-sustaining, dynamic system, constantly folding in on itself, much like the serpent of the Ouroboros. In this sense, the ancient symbol may not just be a metaphor for cycles in nature but an intuitive glimpse into the very mechanics of the cosmos.

The symbolism of the Ouroboros also extends to personal transformation. In alchemy, the serpent eating its own tail was associated with the *magnum opus*, the great work of spiritual and material refinement. The alchemists believed that just as base metals could be transformed into gold, the human soul could be purified and reborn through self-destruction and renewal. The Ouroboros, in this context, was a reminder that true transformation requires a complete dissolution of the self before something new can emerge.

But why would this symbol emerge in so many different cultures? One possibility is that it was a remnant of an older, now-forgotten civilization, a knowledge system passed down through various cultural expressions. Some researchers believe that the echoes of the Ouroboros may trace back to lost teachings from a prehistoric world, possibly from an advanced society that predates written history.

Another perspective is that the Ouroboros is not something learned but something *remembered*—a fundamental truth that all human beings, regardless of time and place, can intuitively grasp. The cycle of life, death, and rebirth is evident in the changing seasons, in the movement of the stars, in the patterns of nature. Perhaps this universal experience is why the symbol arises independently across civilizations, as a way to articulate something deeply embedded in human consciousness.

There is also a psychological dimension to the Ouroboros. Carl Jung, the Swiss psychologist, saw it as a symbol of individuation, the process by which a person integrates the conscious and unconscious mind. He believed that the Ouroboros represented the self-reflective nature of human thought—the idea that we must confront and consume our own illusions, our own fears, in order to evolve. In this sense, the Ouroboros is not just a cosmic symbol but a deeply personal one.

If the Ouroboros holds a hidden truth, it is this: nothing ever truly ends. Everything transforms, everything renews. The cycle is endless, but it is not meaningless. It suggests that destruction is not final, that death is not an end, that even when something appears to be consumed, it is only the beginning of something new. Whether applied to the universe, to personal growth, or to the mysteries of existence, the Ouroboros reminds us that the journey never truly stops.

But if this is true—if the Ouroboros is more than just a mythological image—then what else have we forgotten? What other truths have been encoded in symbols, waiting for those who are willing to see? Perhaps the Ouroboros is not just a relic of the past, but a key to understanding something that has always been right before our eyes.

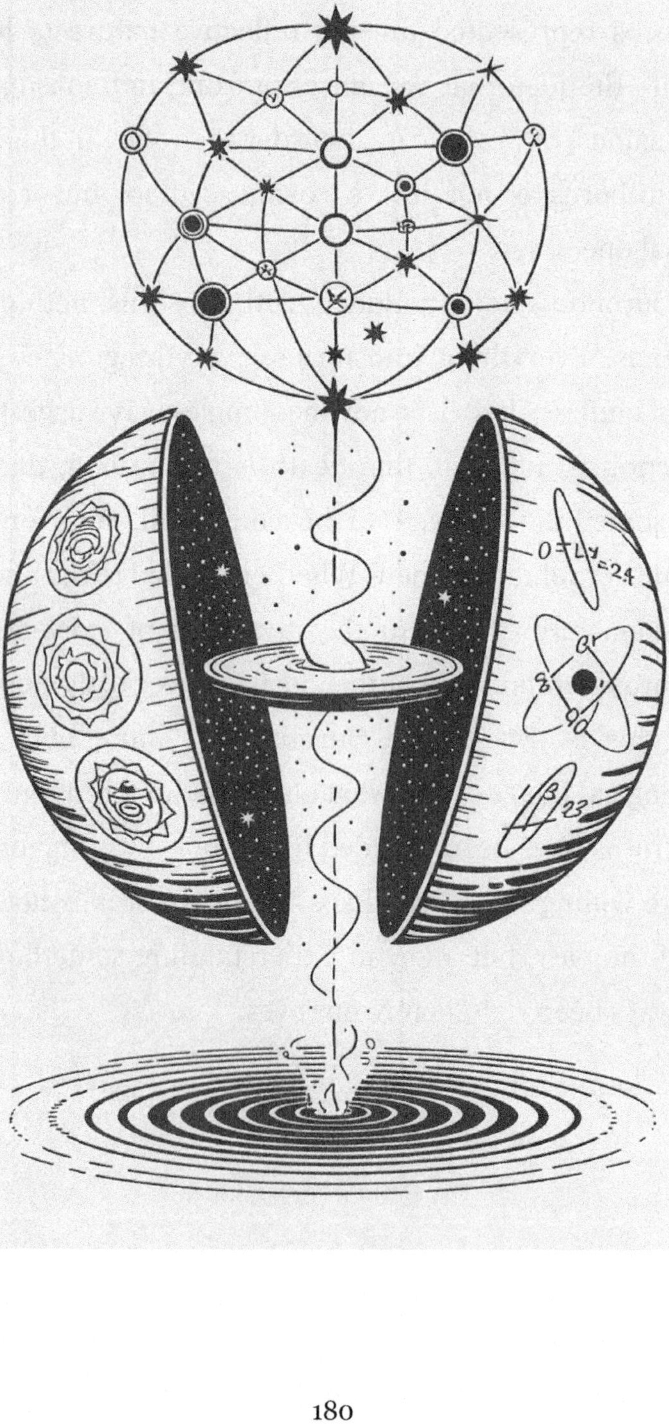

29. The *science of consciousness* is now catching up to ancient wisdom: quantum physics suggests that *all things are connected,* mirroring the esoteric idea of *oneness.*

For centuries, mystics, sages, and philosophers have spoken of an underlying unity that connects all things. They have described reality not as a collection of separate objects, but as a single, interconnected whole, where everything influences everything else. This idea, central to ancient spiritual traditions, has long been dismissed by the rational mind as mystical speculation, a poetic but ultimately unscientific view of the universe. But now, modern physics—particularly in the field of quantum mechanics—is beginning to echo what these traditions have always known: that separation is an illusion, and at the most fundamental level, all things are connected.

The idea of oneness is woven into countless spiritual and esoteric traditions. In Hinduism, the concept of *Brahman* describes a singular, infinite reality that underlies all existence. In Taoism, the *Tao* is seen as the formless essence that flows through and unites all things. The Hermetic axiom *as above, so below* suggests that everything is a reflection of a greater whole. Gnostic texts speak of the *pleroma*, a boundless totality from which all things emerge. In Buddhism, the doctrine of *interdependent origination* teaches that nothing exists in isolation, that everything is part of a vast web of relationships. These traditions, spanning cultures and centuries, all point to the same fundamental truth: that reality is not made up of independent parts but of interwoven patterns of energy and consciousness.

For much of human history, science and spirituality have been seen as opposing forces. Science sought to explain the material world through observation and measurement, while spirituality explored the unseen, the immeasurable. Yet, with the rise of quantum physics, the boundary between these two perspectives has begun to blur. The discoveries of the past century have challenged the classical view of a mechanistic universe, replacing it with something far stranger, something that aligns more closely with the ancient vision of reality as a unified whole.

One of the most astonishing findings in quantum mechanics is the phenomenon of entanglement. When two particles become entangled, they remain connected no matter how far apart they are. A change in one particle is instantly reflected in the other, even if they are separated by vast distances. This defies the conventional understanding of space and time, suggesting that information can travel instantaneously across the universe, or that space itself may not be as absolute as once thought. To the mystic, this is not surprising. It is merely confirmation of what has always been known—that all things are one, and that separateness is only an illusion.

Quantum superposition is another revelation that aligns with esoteric teachings. A quantum particle does not exist in a single state until it is observed; rather, it exists in all possible states simultaneously. This mirrors the mystical idea that reality is shaped by consciousness, that the universe does not take form independently of the observer but is, in some way, a projection of awareness itself. The ancient sages who taught that *the world is but a dream* may have been closer to the truth than anyone imagined.

Perhaps the most significant implication of quantum mechanics is that consciousness itself may be fundamental to reality. The famous double-slit experiment revealed that the mere act of observation changes the behavior of particles, suggesting that consciousness is not separate from the physical world but an integral part of it. Some physicists have even proposed that the universe may be a vast, conscious system, that what we perceive as matter is merely a manifestation of a deeper, underlying intelligence.

If this is true, then what does it say about the nature of human consciousness? Could it be that we are not isolated beings, not individual minds trapped within separate bodies, but part of a greater field of awareness? Mystical traditions have long described consciousness as a vast ocean, with each individual mind being like a wave rising and falling within it. The boundaries between self and other, between subject and object, may be far more fluid than they appear.

This view is supported by studies in neuroscience and psychology. Research into altered states of consciousness, whether induced by meditation, psychedelics, or near-death experiences, suggests that when the ordinary sense of self dissolves, what remains is not emptiness, but a profound sense of unity. Those who have undergone such experiences often report a feeling of being connected to everything, as if their awareness extends beyond the confines of their body and merges with the fabric of existence itself.

If consciousness is fundamental, then reality is not something that exists independently of us. It is something we participate in, something we help create. This idea is not new. Many esoteric traditions have long taught that the mind shapes the world, that intention and thought influence reality in ways that science is only now beginning to explore. The power of words, of symbols, of focused intention—all of these have been used for centuries in spiritual practices to manifest change. What quantum physics suggests is that this may not be superstition at all, but a real principle woven into the structure of the universe.

This also raises profound questions about the nature of free will. If reality is shaped by consciousness, then to what extent are we responsible for the world we experience? If everything is interconnected, then every thought, every action, every moment of awareness contributes to the whole. This perspective transforms the way we see ourselves and our place in the universe. We are not separate from the cosmos. We *are* the cosmos, expressing itself as human beings.

But if science is now catching up to what ancient wisdom has always taught, then why has this knowledge been suppressed for so long? Why has the idea of oneness been replaced with a worldview of division, of separation, of conflict? Is it possible that those who benefit from control have a vested interest in keeping humanity from realizing its true nature? If consciousness is powerful, if reality is malleable, then what happens when people awaken to their own ability to shape it? Perhaps this is why mystical traditions have always been pushed to the margins of society. Perhaps this is why those who have taught the power of the mind, of unity, of inner transformation, have so often been persecuted. A population that understands its own power, that recognizes its fundamental connection to all things, is far more difficult to control than one that believes in separation, in scarcity, in fear.

If quantum physics is revealing what ancient wisdom has always known, then what comes next? What happens when humanity fully embraces the idea that we are not just observers of the universe, but participants in its unfolding? If the world is a reflection of consciousness, then changing the world begins not with external actions, but with a shift in awareness.

The path forward is not about rejecting science or abandoning reason. It is about expanding our understanding of what science truly is. The search for knowledge, for truth, does not belong solely to laboratories and equations. It belongs to every human being who has ever looked inward, who has ever questioned the nature of existence, who has ever felt that there is something more. And now, as science and spirituality converge, as the old barriers between matter and mind begin to dissolve, the question is no longer whether all things are connected. The question is: what will we do with this knowledge?

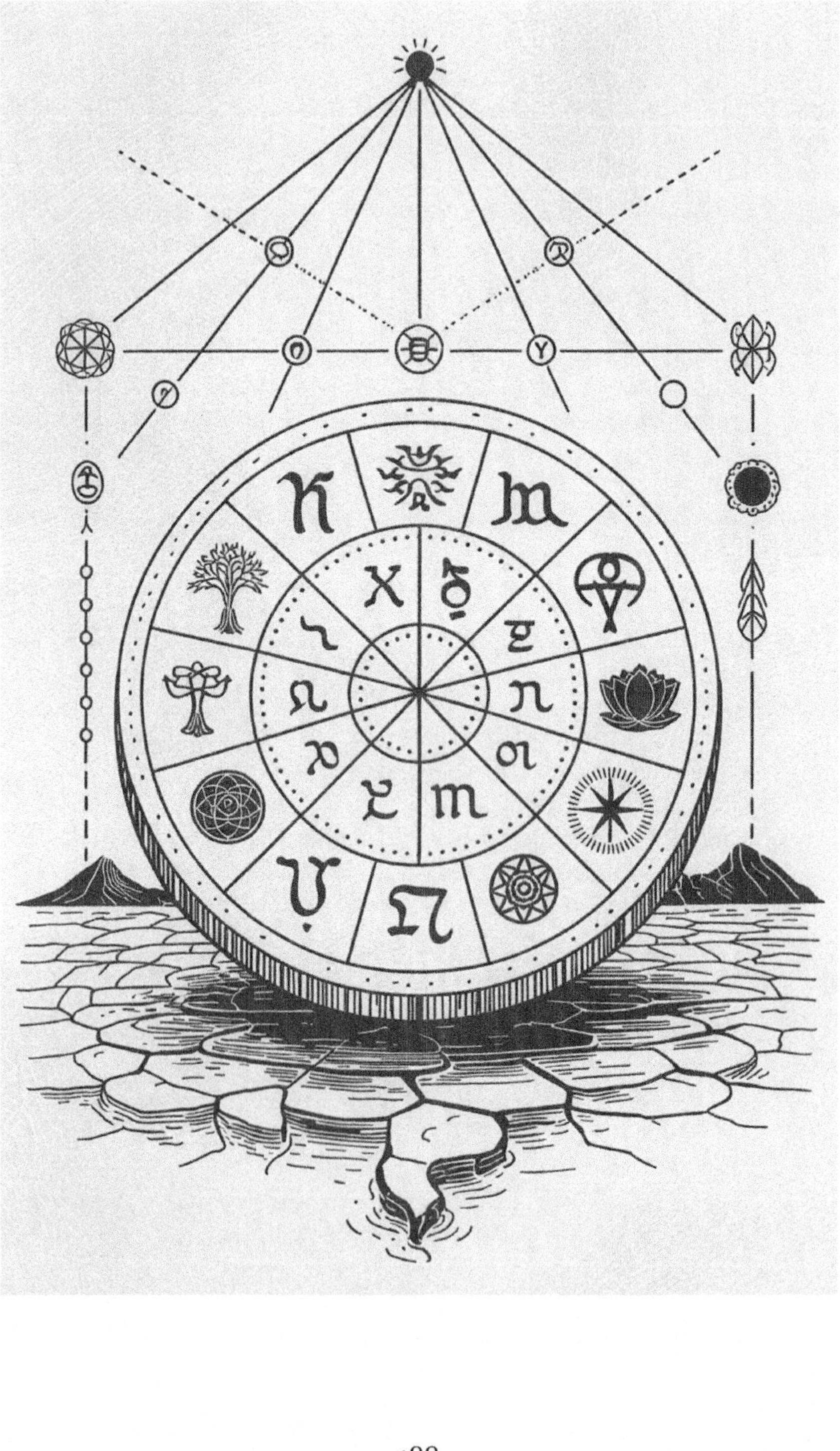

30. The *12 Universal Laws*, passed down through Hermeticism, Vedanta, Kabbalah, and Gnosticism, offer a framework for understanding *the hidden mechanics of reality.*

For thousands of years, mystics, philosophers, and esoteric scholars have spoken of hidden laws that govern reality—principles that shape existence not only in the physical world but in the realms of mind and spirit. These laws, preserved in Hermeticism, Vedanta, Kabbalah, and Gnosticism, have been whispered through the corridors of secret societies, encoded in sacred texts, and passed down through traditions that seek to unveil the deeper workings of the universe. Though their expressions may vary, their essence remains the same: the cosmos is not random, nor is it ruled by blind chance. It moves according to patterns, rhythms, and laws—twelve fundamental principles that underlie everything we experience.

The first of these, the Law of Mentalism, declares that all is mind. Reality, at its core, is not material but mental. The universe itself is consciousness unfolding, and everything within it is a projection of thought. This idea, central to Hermetic teachings, finds echoes in modern quantum physics, which suggests that observation shapes the world at the most fundamental level. If everything is mind, then perception is not just passive—it is creative. What we focus on, we bring into being. This is the foundation upon which all the other laws rest.

The Law of Correspondence reflects the ancient maxim, *as above, so below; as within, so without.* It teaches that the same principles operate on every level of reality, from the microcosm of the individual to the macrocosm of the universe. The structure of an atom mirrors that of a solar system. The cycles of nature reflect the cycles of human thought. What happens in the outer world is a reflection of what happens within. This principle is a key to understanding synchronicity, the phenomenon where events align in seemingly meaningful ways, revealing the hidden order beneath apparent chaos.

The Law of Vibration states that nothing rests, that everything is in constant motion. Even what appears solid is, at the atomic level, a field of vibrating energy. Every thought, every emotion, every state of being carries its own frequency. High vibrations align with love, clarity, and truth. Low vibrations manifest as fear, confusion, and disharmony. By understanding this law, we recognize that we are not static beings but dynamic fields of energy, constantly interacting with and influencing the frequencies around us.

The Law of Polarity teaches that everything has its opposite, yet opposites are not truly separate—they are two ends of the same spectrum. Light and darkness, heat and cold, joy and sorrow—each is a variation of the other. By understanding polarity, we gain mastery over our emotions and experiences. Instead of being controlled by extremes, we learn to shift from one state to another with awareness. The difference between fear and courage is simply a matter of degree.

The Law of Rhythm reminds us that everything moves in cycles. The tides rise and fall. The seasons change. Planets follow predictable orbits. Even human emotions and societal patterns move through phases. Nothing is permanent, and this understanding brings both humility and empowerment. When we recognize the rhythms of life, we learn to flow with them rather than resist them. Difficult times are not endless; they are part of a greater cycle that will eventually turn.

The Law of Cause and Effect, known in the East as karma, reveals that nothing happens by accident. Every action sets in motion a chain of reactions. Thoughts, words, and deeds ripple outward, shaping our reality. This law is not about punishment or reward—it is about alignment. When we act in harmony with truth, the effects bring growth and expansion. When we act in ignorance, the effects bring lessons meant to awaken us.

The Law of Gender speaks to the balance of forces within all things. Masculine and feminine energies exist not only in biology but in every aspect of life. The active and the receptive, the creative and the sustaining—each plays a role in the dance of existence. Neither is superior; both are necessary. This law teaches that integration, rather than dominance, is the path to true power.

Beyond these foundational principles, the remaining Universal Laws further refine the workings of reality. The Law of Perpetual Transmutation states that energy is always moving, always changing form. Nothing is truly stagnant. Even the heaviest situations contain the potential for transformation. The Law of Compensation ensures that energy is never lost—what is given is returned, though not always in the way one expects. The Law of Relativity teaches that all things are measured in comparison; no situation is good or bad on its own, but only in relation to another. The Law of Divine Oneness underscores that all things are interconnected, that nothing exists in isolation. The Law of Attraction, perhaps the most widely known, expresses that like attracts like—our internal state determines what we draw into our lives.

Together, these twelve laws form a blueprint for understanding existence. They are not imposed by any external force; they are intrinsic to the fabric of reality itself. When we align with them, life flows with greater ease. When we resist them, we encounter struggle—not as a form of punishment, but as a signal that we are out of harmony with the natural order.

Why, then, has this knowledge been obscured? Why are these laws not widely taught? Perhaps because to understand them fully is to realize that power over one's life does not come from external sources. It does not come from governments, religions, or institutions. It comes from within. To grasp these laws is to awaken to the fact that reality is not something that happens *to* us but something we are actively participating in at all times.

If the universe is mental, then thought is the architect of reality. If everything corresponds, then nothing is random. If vibration governs all things, then what we choose to resonate with shapes our destiny. If polarity teaches that opposites are one, then the conflicts of the world are but illusions of separation. If rhythm reminds us that all things pass, then no struggle is eternal. If cause and effect are absolute, then every action holds weight. If gender exists in all things, then balance is the key to wholeness.

These are not just abstract ideas. They are practical tools. When understood deeply, they change how one interacts with life itself. They shift perspective, dissolving victimhood, replacing it with clarity and responsibility. They show that we are not at the mercy of unseen forces—we *are* the force, shaping reality through awareness, intention, and action.

Perhaps this is why these laws have been preserved across different traditions. The Hermeticists encoded them in their writings, knowing that only those ready to understand would seek them out. The Vedantic sages spoke of them through parables, guiding seekers toward realization. The Kabbalists wove them into mystical teachings, offering keys to those who could decipher their meaning. The Gnostics hinted at them, knowing that the truth could not be imposed—it had to be recognized.

If reality operates by laws, then ignorance of them does not protect one from their effects. A person unaware of gravity still falls if they step off a ledge. So too, those unaware of these deeper laws still experience their consequences. The difference is that those who understand can work with them consciously, rather than being pushed and pulled by unseen forces.

The twelve Universal Laws do not demand belief. They simply *are*. Like gravity, like magnetism, like the motion of the planets, they function regardless of human awareness. But for those who see them, for those who recognize their presence, they offer something invaluable—the ability to move through life with a sense of mastery, to engage with the world not as a victim of fate but as a participant in creation.

And so the question is not whether these laws exist. The question is whether we are willing to see them. Whether we are ready to align with the hidden mechanics of reality, to step beyond the illusion of randomness, and to embrace the knowledge that has always been waiting.

Conclusion

The past is never truly lost. It lingers beneath the surface, waiting to be remembered. The knowledge explored in these pages is not new—it has whispered through the ages, concealed in symbols, woven into myths, buried in texts that were dismissed or destroyed. It has survived because truth cannot be erased, only obscured. And even when forgotten, it finds ways to return.

History moves in cycles. Civilizations rise, knowledge flourishes, then power intervenes. Ideas are silenced, books are burned, and what was once sacred becomes heresy. But the cycle does not end there. Suppression breeds curiosity, and curiosity leads to rediscovery. What was dismissed as legend is reexamined, what was outlawed is revived. The wisdom of the ancients was never truly lost—it was simply hidden, waiting for the right moment to reemerge.

Perhaps that moment is now.

Science is beginning to catch up to what mystics have always known. Consciousness shapes reality. The universe is not a cold machine, but something alive, something interconnected. The energy of thought, the power of symbols, the hidden laws that govern existence—these are not fantasies, but forces we are only beginning to understand. If ancient civilizations held the keys to these truths, why were they silenced? If the esoteric teachings carried knowledge so profound, why were they forbidden?

And if this knowledge has been rediscovered time and time again, then what else is still hidden? What remains just beyond the edge of memory, waiting for those who are willing to see?

Not everything can be answered in a book. Some truths must be lived, experienced, *remembered*. Perhaps that is why this knowledge was never meant to be given freely—because it is not in the words themselves, but in the way they awaken something within. A distant echo, a recognition, a knowing that defies logic.

What if you were never meant to *learn* these truths, but to *remember* them?

Made in the USA
Coppell, TX
02 May 2025